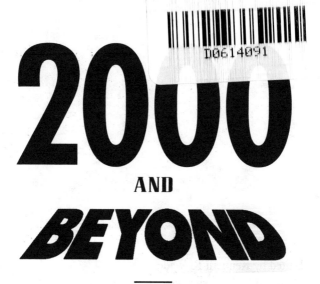

2000
AND
BEYOND

MARK FINLEY

Pacific Press Publishing Association
Boise, Idaho
Oshawa, Ontario, Canada

Edited by Kenneth R. Wade
Designed by Michelle Petz
Cover art by Lars Justinen

Copyright © 1996 by
Pacific Press Publishing Association
Printed in the United States of America
All Rights Reserved

Bible texts quoted are from the King James Version unless otherwise noted.

ISBN 0-8163-1361-X

96 97 98 99 00 • 5 4 3 2 1

Contents

Someone has well said, "You can live days without food, hours without water, minutes without air, but only seconds without hope." Hope buoys our spirits. It keeps us alive. In this chapter you will be encouraged by the greatest hope in the universe—a hope that will lift your courage and send your spirits soaring.

CHAPTER ONE

A Fresh Breath of Hope

As I dashed through the checkout counter in our local grocery store, I paused long enough to catch the headline of a tabloid newspaper. It was just a casual glance. Then I looked again and again, my eyes now riveted on the words. Let me assure you, I'm no tabloid newspaper buff. In my view, the tabloids are cheap, sensational junk for gullible people who will read just about anything. But these headlines were different. Bold letters, spread from one margin to the other, proclaimed: BIBLE PREDICTIONS FOR 1996. I couldn't resist. I bought the paper. According to the tabloid, here are the Bible predictions for 1996:

- Hundreds of millions will convert to Christianity on February 19, 1996.
- Record heat and drought will occur in March,

leading to worldwide food shortages in 1996.

- The collapse of the European Common Market will lead to the rise of the Antichrist in Western Europe in the summer of '96.
- A mile-high image of Jesus will appear over Washington, D.C., after a thunderstorm in July of 1996, leading thousands more to conversion.
- An evangelist will ascend to heaven while preaching to thousands in Dallas in 1996. This whole event will be captured on video.
- The four horsemen of the Apocalypse will be sighted outside Montreal in July of '96 and sighted again outside Copenhagen in August.

It's fascinating that an article about Bible prophecies, which will be read and believed by thousands, doesn't have one Bible text in support. The devil has had a field day deceiving gullible people. Why would a tabloid newspaper print an article on Bible predictions for 1996? There is only one answer—to sell newspapers. The bottom line is profit margin.

Tabloid newspaper editors realize that there's been a worldwide explosion of interest in the second coming of Christ. Increasing numbers of people believe that as we approach the year 2000, the end of the world is on its way. The tabloids have chosen to capitalize on this.

Gerald Celente, the director of Trends Research Institute in Rhinebeck, New York, calls this "millennium fever." He says,

> Today as we head toward another millennium, growing numbers of ordinary people look around

the world and see troubling times. Anxious and confused, they are worried about the course of events and where they'll lead. They see reports of the incurable Ebola virus spreading in Zaire, the resurgence of pneumonia plague in India, the slaughter of hundreds of thousands in Yugoslavia, the ongoing massacre of millions in Africa, escalating wars in the former Soviet Union, and frightening new levels of terrorism in the United States.

Even President Clinton finds the times troubling. He made history when he ordered Pennsylvania Avenue permanently closed in front of the White House to deter a potential car or truck bomb attack. These and other unsettling events are the grist for the doomsday mill: a world spinning out of control and an impending calamity.

As the year 2000 approaches, more and more prophets of doom predict that worsening conditions will herald in the beginning of the end. All of this speculation regarding the year 2000, the time of the end, and the second coming of Christ leads us to some basic questions. Is there a word from the Lord in this last decade of our millennium? Is there some message from the Almighty for this hour? Is there something that God Himself wants to say to us?

The Promise of His Return

One thing is for certain, the Bible is filled with promises of the second coming of Christ. References to the event appear at least 1500 times in Scripture—once in every 25 verses in the New Testament. David declared it when he said, "Our God shall come, and shall not keep silence: a fire shall devour before him, and it shall be very tempestuous round about him" (Psalm 50:3). Paul echoed it as he declared, "The Lord Himself shall descend from heaven with a shout, with the voice of the archangel, and with the trump of God: and the dead in Christ shall rise first" (1 Thessalonians 4:16). The angels affirmed it. As the disciples strained their necks and squinted their eyes, looking longingly into heaven at the ascension of Christ, two angels standing by said, "Ye men of Galilee, why stand ye gazing up into heaven? this same Jesus, which is taken up from you into heaven, shall so come in like manner as ye have seen him go" (Acts 1:11).

Christ Himself promised it when He assured His disciples, "Let not your heart be troubled: ye believe in God, believe also in me. In my Father's house are many mansions: if it were not so, I would have told you. I go to prepare a place for you. And if I go and prepare a place for you, I will come again, and receive you unto myself; that where I am, there ye may be also" (John 14:1-3).

The Answer to Loneliness

The second coming of Christ is the ultimate answer to loneliness, low self-esteem, hopelessness, and despair. Deep within every human heart is the desire to love and be loved. The desire for companionship. We were not made to be alone.

Scientists studying rats noted that mother rats often lick their young. At first they thought this might be some form of bathing. The more they studied the phenomenon, however, the more they came to the conclusion that the mother rat was not bathing her babies at all. Rather, she was love-licking them. The licking was a form of kissing or embracing. Further research revealed that when baby rats are separated from their mothers and provided all the essentials of life, they die at much quicker rates than when they are love-licked by their mothers. The scientists have come to the conclusion that baby rats must be licked in love in order to survive. This licking provides a sense of security . . . a sense of belonging . . . a sense of identity. The ultimate answer to loneliness is this sense of caring.

Every one of us has this longing to be loved unconditionally. To be accepted no matter who we are, where we've come from, what we've done. Revelation 21:3 affirms that one day we will be with God. We were made for Him. He will fill the empty loneliness of our lives. "Behold, the tabernacle of God is with men, and he will dwell with them, and they shall be his people, and God himself shall be with them, and be their God."

Looking toward a future that is bright with the promises of God, today I have a place to belong, today I have hope in my despair. Because I am valuable to Him, today I have reason to feel good about myself. One day I will see Him face to face and be licked by the love of God. He has promised never to forsake me, and although I cannot see Him today, His second coming reassures me that, one day soon, I will.

The Answer to the Problem of Pain

The second coming of Christ is also the answer to the problem of pain, suffering, sorrow, and tears. At cancer wards across the country, patients have had their bodies weakened through multiple surgeries, chemotherapy, and radiation therapy. They've lost their hair, their weight, their strength, and some have lost the will to live. When your body is racked with pain so intense that you can hardly think,when you've dealt with the grief and the anger and the fear, when you've wrestled through the question, "Why me, Lord?" true comfort can be found in the second coming of Christ.

Revelation 21:4 discusses the year 2000 and beyond. It describes God's plan for every one of His children after our Lord's return. "And God shall wipe away all tears from their eyes; and there shall be no more death, neither sorrow, nor crying, neither shall there be any more pain: for the former things are passed away."

Come with me to Rwanda. Hutus and Tutsis are at war. Thousands have been massacred, blood flows freely in the streets. The human tide of refugees clogs the roads, and some have been trampled to death. Some of the refugee camps have become death camps. The food shortage is acute.

Come with me to the former Yugoslavia. Consider the untold story of the human suffering on all sides in that war. The intensity of human pain, the epidemic of human suffering, and the rivers of human tears cry out for it all to end.

The second coming of Christ is the ultimate answer to the problem of human suffering. It's the only answer to the world's agonizing pain, and it's the only solution for your tears as well.

When you suffer, when your body is racked with pain, when you can't stand it another day, when your eyes are filled with tears, you can hope again. You can look away from your suffering because you know that despite it all, there is a God who still loves you and one day He will put an end to all heart disease, cancer, and pain. One day death will be over. One day all the suffering will be forgotten.

The second coming of Christ enables us to hope again. It is the ultimate solution to the loneliness. It is the ultimate solution to low self-esteem. Someone loves you. He loves you so much that He's preparing a marvelous future for you.

He's coming back again to take you to your true home.

The second coming of Christ is the ultimate solution to the problem of suffering, pain, and tears. One day Christ will give us new bodies that will pulsate with life and joy and health. He will take us to a land where there is no suffering or heartache or sickness or sorrow and death.

The Answer to the Problem of Injustice

The second coming of Jesus is the ultimate answer to the problem of injustice. In Revelation 21:5, the Lord says, "I make all things new." Where is fairness when your husband leaves you for another woman? You have raised your children together. They're married and out of the home. Now he is gone, and you are left with this agonizing loneliness. Where is justice when a drunk driver kills your seventeen-year-old daughter? Where is justice when you've lived a decent life and you get cancer while your drinking, smoking, drug-abusing neighbor seems to be healthy? Where is justice when you've worked for the same company for twenty years and then they lay you off?

This life is filled with injustice. It's filled with unfairness. But one day the King of Righteousness will reign. Christ will sit upon His heavenly throne. In eternity, society will be fair and just and right. We may not be treated fairly here, but we will be then. Justice may not always be found on earth, but it will be found in heaven. It may not always be meted out by man, but it will be given to us by God. When you have been treated unfairly, look beyond the injustice to the kingdom of God, when all things will be set straight. When you've been treated unjustly, look beyond the hurt to God's new society, where He will reign in righteousness.

When Joan Herman was seventeen years old, she radiated with the idealism of youth. She spent the summer of 1948 working in a Quaker work camp as a volunteer. Her great desire was to help the mountain people of Pennsylvania improve the quality of their lives. Along with other workers, she participated in digging irrigation ditches to bring running water to some of their remote areas. The summer of 1948, a polio epidemic swept across the midwestern and eastern United States. Joanie's symptoms started simply at first—a cold, fever, chills, sweats, muscle pain, and then fatigue. Soon she could hardly stand it. The pain in her back became unbearable. She often leaned over her shovel and pushed against the warm earth in the ditch she was digging. Rubbing her back against the drainage ditch wall seemed to give her pain some relief. One day, seized with intense pain, she collapsed. The diagnosis was polio. Ultimately, Joanie was paralyzed from her neck down. Her physicians placed her in a large pressurized cylinder with only her head sticking out. Since her lungs had totally collapsed, this "iron lung" was the only way to maintain her breathing. After living twenty years in this condition, Joanie developed cancer.

I had the opportunity to visit Joanie on numerous occasions. Her experience did not make her bitter, it only made her hopeful. It did not make her angry, it only made her eager for the coming of the Lord. Joanie's mind was fixed on one event. She clung to a single promise, the promise of our Lord when He said, "I will come again." She cheered the other physically handicapped people around her because the hope of the second coming of Christ buoyed her up. Joanie was filled with hopeful anticipation of the second advent. She was not filled with anger at the apparent injustice of a seventeen-year-old getting polio. She was able to look beyond the pain, the suffering, and the agony of her life to the day when God would bring fairness and justice to the universe.

Cancer is unfair, but one day it will be done away with. War is unfair, but one day it will end. Poverty is unfair, but one day there will be prosperity for all. Famine is unfair, but one day there will be abundance. We can hope again because this earth is not the end of the road. And God ultimately will set all things right.

The Answer to the Problems of Aging and Death

The second coming of Christ is the ultimate answer to the problems of aging and death. No wrinkle-free cream will keep you from aging. No cosmetic surgery will stop the years from marching by. No eyelid job or eye-bag operation will keep you looking young forever. There is no magic potion or magic formula. Hair transplants to combat baldness won't do it. Everyone in this life is born and dies. It is a reality.

Throughout history, Christians and non-Christians have faced death in different ways. In the catacombs, the inscriptions in the pagan tombs read something like this: "Goodbye forever, my love." The Christian inscriptions, on the other hand, are much more hopeful: "Goodbye until the morning." Christians never meet for the last time. There is a wonderful, glorious reunion day coming. When a baby is stillborn, it's not goodbye forever, but goodbye until the morning. When a teenager is killed in an auto collision, it's not goodbye forever but goodbye until the morning. When a middle-aged man dies from a heart attack, it's not goodbye forever, but goodbye until the morning. When a young mother is afflicted with breast cancer and dies, it's not goodbye forever, but goodbye until the morning. The apostle Paul describes that triumphant morning in these words:

> Behold, I shew you a mystery; We shall not all sleep, but we shall all be changed, in a moment, in the twinkling of an eye, at the last trump: for the trumpet shall sound, and the dead shall be raised incorruptible, and we shall be changed. . . . Then shall be brought to pass the saying that is written, Death is swallowed up in victory (1 Cor. 15:51, 54).

Have you lost a loved one by death? Have you laid a child to rest on some grassy hillside? Has your husband, your wife, your son, or daughter been stricken with a fatal disease? Does the grief seem too much to bear alone? You don't have to bear it alone. Jesus will carry it for you today and point you to a future where it will be no more.

The morning will bring the realization of our hope. The morning will bring a great new society. The morning will usher in the second coming of Jesus Christ. Through your bouts of loneliness, you can hope again—Christ is coming. Through your moments of discouragement, you can hope again—Christ is coming. Through the pain of physical suffering, you can hope again—Christ is coming. Through the disappointment of injustices, you can hope again—Christ is coming. Through the tears of the loss of your loved one, you can hope again—for our Lord is returning.

It is obvious that something is wrong with our planet. Instability is increasing worldwide. Natural disasters, deteriorating world conditions, and rising crime and violence shout at us, "Something is wrong!" But there is a solution. You'll discover it as you understand Revelation's end-time omens.

CHAPTER TWO

Revelation's End-Time Surprises

When the sun is shining brightly in the clear blue Colombian sky, the flight into the interior town of Cali can be spectacular. The approach through lush valleys bordered by the towering Andes is breathtaking. In stormy weather on an overcast, rain-drenched night, the scene changes dramatically. Reporter John Ritter of *USA Today* describes it as "driving through a tunnel blindfolded" (*USA Today*, 18 January 1996). Even with the aircraft's flight computer operating at peak efficiency, threading a safe corridor through the mountain peaks is challenging. The last thing an English-speaking pilot needs is to experience communication difficulties with the air-traffic controller.

On December 20, 1995, an American Airlines flight approached Cali on an extremely foggy night. Unusual downdrafts made navigation difficult. Then it happened . . . a pilot's worst fear . . . *the flight controller misunderstood the message from the cockpit. His instructions to the pilot were confusing.* The plane banked left instead of right. Instantly, it smashed into the face of the towering mountains, killing all 160 people on board. Although the air-traffic controller's error was not the only factor in the fatal crash of American Airlines Flight 965, it was certainly a decisive one.

Confused instructions . . . a garbled signal . . . a misunderstood message ended in a tragic fatality. In our spiritual lives, listening to a false message can be equally devastating, particularly as we approach the end of earth's history. The psychics, astrologers, and spiritualists speak confidently about the future, but their track record is poor. A careful evaluation reveals that their predictions are way off the mark more often than they are on target. Accepting their message will only lead to a spiritual disaster. Millions, unfortunately, accept their falsehoods and receive a garbled message about which way to turn.

We're nearing the end of the journey. Spacecraft Earth is about to touch down. Final descent just before landing is the most treacherous part. The fog is thick. The mountains are high. Our only safety is following our divine Air-Traffic Controller. There are plenty of voices waiting to send us erroneous messages. Jesus, Himself, is the only one who clearly outlines the signs and end-time omens that will precede His return.

The Bible's amazing predictions regarding these last days are clear. Some of these predictions may surprise you. Here are four detailed predictions of end-time events:

Prediction 1

World leaders will discuss peace, while world events become increasingly unstable. The threat of nuclear war will continually increase as the knowledge of how to

build a nuclear bomb and the material needed to build it become more available (see Matthew 24:6, 7; Revelation 11:18; 1 Thessalonians 5:3).

Have you noticed how fragile peace treaties are these days? Shortly after signing the cease-fire accord with the British government, the Irish Republican Army reconsidered. On February 12, 1996, at 7:01 p.m. London time, a mighty explosion rocked the city's south end. Seventeen people died. A few days later, another bomb exploded in a London bus, killing and maiming even more people. Peace once again gave way to violence. Marches in the streets of Sarajevo and most of former Yugoslavia threatened the Dayton Peace Accord. The Middle East is a tinderbox waiting to explode. The untimely assassination of Prime Minister Yitzhak Rabin threatened to undo the Arab-Israeli Peace Process.

Speaking of our time, the apostle Paul declared, "When they shall say, Peace and safety; then sudden destruction cometh upon them . . . and they shall not escape" (1 Thessalonians 5:3).

The reason there is war in the streets is because there is war in our hearts. Conflict within leads to conflict without. Peace treaties fail because they are based on frail human promises. When Jesus, the Prince of Peace, fills the heart with His peace, it makes a dramatic difference.

Although the Strategic Arms Limitation talks have produced an agreement between the superpowers to destroy a percentage of their nuclear arsenal, the world is more unsafe today than it was a few years ago. With the breakup of the former Soviet Union into the Commonwealth of Independent States, the nuclear arsenal is actually less secure. On March 23, 1992, *U.S. News & World Report* noted that a "high-ranking officer in Moscow has confirmed a U.S. Intelligence report that three tactical nuclear weapons have vanished from a former Red Army

Arsenal in Kazakhstan" (p. 26). Sources speculated that these three nuclear warheads were sold to Iran. The April 6, 1992, edition of the same magazine quoted Russian general Viktor Samolikov as saying, "Too many unauthorized persons have access to the nuclear storage sites" (p. 22).

Nuclear weapons are much more accessible today. The January 1996 issue of *Popular Mechanics* states, "If you were planning to build a nuclear bomb, you would probably want to visit your local library to read such classics as *Los Alamos Primer: First Lectures On How To Build An Atomic Bomb*. Although not exactly a blueprint, the book is considered a good guide to the physics of nuclear fission. Saddam Hussein's bomb development team had a copy in its library. You can obtain one for $27.50 by calling the University of California Press."

What if a terrorist group develops a nuclear bomb? Would it be possible to use nuclear weapons to hold the rest of the world hostage? The more bombs that are built, the greater the possibility one will explode through madness or sheer folly. Although the United States and the former Soviet Union are dismantling a portion of their nuclear arsenal, nations such as India, Pakistan, Iran, Iraq, and North Korea are quietly building up theirs.

As if the nuclear threat alone was not bad enough, the word is now in that Libya is building the world's largest chemical weapons factory.

Jesus pointed forward to our day when He emphatically declared, "Men's hearts [will be] failing them from fear and the expectation of those things which are coming on the earth, for the powers of heaven will be shaken" (Luke 21:26, NKJV). Was our Saviour describing a limited nuclear holocaust when He warned there will be "fearful sights and great signs" in the heavens? (Luke 21:11).

Revelation, the Bible's last book, contains probably the most graphic description of the threat of nuclear war preceding the final climax of all human history. "The nations were angry, and thy wrath is come, and the time of the dead, that they should be judged, and that thou shouldest give reward unto thy servants the prophets, and to the saints, and them that fear thy name, small and great; and shouldest destroy them which destroy the earth" (Revelation 11:18).

Christ will return at a time when the human race has the capacity for self-destruction. He will come at a time when world leaders are discussing peace but arming for war. He will return at a time of growing national instability. His return will come at the precise moment in history when the human race stands poised on the verge of annihilation. God's great good news is saturated with hope. This world will not be destroyed in some final nuclear explosion. Christ will return before mankind can reduce our planet to a spinning globe of ash. Help is on its way. We can be certain of that.

Prediction 2

Moral conditions in society will rapidly deteriorate. Crime will rise. Divorce rates will soar. And corruption will become even more widespread (see Matthew 24:12, 38, 39; Genesis 6:5, 11; 2 Timothy 3:1).

Even a casual view of what's going on in our society indicates that something is tragically amiss. When an incorrect turn on a Los Angeles street leads to the shooting of a two-year-old girl by a gun-toting gang protecting its turf, something is drastically wrong with our society. When a disturbed teenager murders his parents, grandparents, and sister because he has had a difficult time adjusting to moving, something is tragically wrong with our society.

Violent crime is creeping like a plague into the once-safe suburbs. Teenage crime is out of control. And it's no wonder. The average child has witnessed 14,000 murders on television by the time he's twelve.

A recent article in *U.S. News & World Report* made this sad commentary: "Disputes once settled with a kiss between kids are now settled with guns. Every hundred hours more youths die in the streets than were killed in the Persian Gulf warfare." American schools have become battlegrounds. Every single year, 6,250 teachers are threatened with bodily injury. Every year, nearly two hundred thousand students skip classes because they fear physical harm.

Jesus clearly outlined the social conditions in our society. In Matthew 27:38, 39, the Saviour compared society's moral conditions in the last days to the days of Noah. What was life like in Noah's day? Spiritual values deteriorated. The ethical pulse of society diminished. Standards that were once the norm, God's standards, were no longer accepted. Genesis 6:1, 2 says that men began to multiply on the face of the earth, perhaps indicating a population explosion like today. "And they took them wives of all which they chose," perhaps indicating rampant divorce. Divorce statistics today are incredible. Consider these staggering facts. In the United States in 1870, there was one divorce for every thirty-four marriages; in 1900, one divorce for every twelve marriages; in 1930, one divorce for every six marriages; in the 1990s, there is one divorce for every two marriages.

Jesus said the morality of society would shrivel and die. Indeed it has. In Luke 17:28-30, Jesus gives us another clue as to what society would be like just before His second coming. "As it was in the days of Lot . . . even thus shall it be in the day when the Son of man is revealed." What was it like in the days of Lot? Lot and his family lived in the infamous city of Sodom. "Sodom and Gomorrah and the surrounding towns gave themselves up to sexual immorality and perversion" (Jude 7, NIV). Other translations of Jude 7 portray the picture even more frankly, stating that "Sodom and Gomorrah indulged in unnatural lust, including the lust of men for other men." Sexual immorality on television and in the movies is common. Extramarital affairs and living together out of wedlock are viewed as normal in today's culture.

The social conditions of our world indicate that we're living on the verge of the kingdom. Christ is soon to return. A new society is on its way. Christ's new kingdom will soon be established.

Prediction 3

Natural disasters will increase. Famines, fires, floods, and earthquakes will rage out of control and become more commonplace (see Matthew 24:7).

Jesus warns us not only of problems in the political world and the social world, but also in the natural world. He plainly foretold, "There shall be famines, and pestilences, and earthquakes, in divers places" (Matthew 24:7). The Bible predicted that all nature would be out of whack, that it would surprise men and women with unusual weather patterns, sudden storms, and devastating hurricanes. Luke 21:25 mentions the roaring sea and waves as a sign. Flash floods will deluge villages and entire cities. The Bible prophesies that these natural disasters will occur in many places.

Famines are commonplace today. Two-thirds of all the children born are in countries that can't supply their food needs. Robert McNamara, former president of the World Bank, says, "Short of nuclear war itself, population growth is the gravest issue the world faces during the next decade.

The sub-Saharan African countries, along with parts of India, are facing dire food shortages. How long will Jesus allow children to die without food? How long can He look down from heaven and see skinny, gaunt bodies, and not come? Jesus must come. Without His return there is no lasting solution to the ravages of starvation. While we, the privileged few, fill our stomachs, millions of others are living with the nearby vultures waiting to eat their flesh. O Lord Jesus, come quickly!

There are strains of disease that are developing a resistance to known antibiotics, and new diseases for which science has not found a cure. In Matthew 24:7, the Bible describes these as "pestilences"—strange diseases on crops or unusual diseases that run rampant through human beings.

The *U.S. News & World Report* for March 23, 1992, carried an article called "The Rape of the Oceans." There now are pestilences in our massive oceans because we're pouring filth into them every day—garbage, raw sewage, toxic wastes. Plankton and other organisms are dying. Radioactive garbage with its deadly potential threatens to make the Chernobyl disaster look like child's play. But, then again, how *do* you dispose of nuclear waste? How *do* you deal with the contamination that comes as a result of nuclear garbage? If Jesus doesn't come soon, we are likely to destroy ourselves. We're living on a planet that's barely retained a hint of its former beauty. It's sick and polluted, and the people on it are self-destructive.

Earthquakes are another example of a prophecy that is being fulfilled. Jesus predicted that there will be great tremblers in these last days. You may wonder, haven't we always had earthquakes? Look at the statistics. Prior to the twentieth century, only ten major earthquakes—only ten big shakers comparable to modern quakes over six on the Richter scale—had been recorded: in Rome, Antioch, China, Jakarta, Tokyo, and the great Lisbon earthquake. When you come to the twentieth century, you find major earthquake after major earthquake.

Certainly there have always been earthquakes, but Jesus warned that earthquakes would now become a noticeable sign. Not only has there been a phenomenal increase, our awareness of them has multiplied greatly as well, due to news reports. There's a whole lot of shaking going on—six thousand earthquakes a year! Christians know why and see it as just one more sign that their Lord will return soon.

The Bible says that all nature will be off its course with earthquakes and other unpredictable things happening. Indeed, they *are* happening. The cover of *Life* magazine says, "Why has nature gone mad?" And *Time* questions, "Was hurricane Andrew a freak, or preview of things to come?" The unstable world conditions, deteriorating morality in our society, and the unpredictable natural disasters reveal that our world is groaning, longing for deliverance, waiting for the coming of Christ.

Prediction 4

Interest in spiritualism, psychic phenomena, and astrology will explode. False revivals will break out like wildfire. There will be a genuine revival of the Spirit. Thousands will be converted. The gospel will rapidly be proclaimed in all the world (see Matthew 24:5, 6; Revelation 14:6; Revelation 18:1; Matthew 24:14).

The Bible predicts a mighty false revival just before the coming of Jesus. There will be increased interest in astrology, psychic phenomena, and communication with the dead. All over the world men and women seem to be interested in the subject of life after death. In the 1970s Ralph Moody, Jr., wrote a book called *Life After Life*. The idea is that when a person dies, he leaves his body, goes through a long tunnel, and at the end of that tunnel meets a glorious being in white. Since that book's publication, interest in contacting the dead has skyrocketed. Over two thousand newspapers in the United States now carry astrology columns. More and more people consult psychics to discover the future. The devil is pulling out all stops in the last days. But God is not caught by surprise. Unusual demonic activity from beneath calls for unprecedented supernatural power from above.

There is another powerful force loose on this planet that is doing its part to hurl us toward the end of the world. It's pushing us toward an impact at the end of time. It's powerful—more powerful than almost anyone realizes. It has a divine, supernatural source. Yet it remains hidden from most people's view. What is this force? No, it's not some New Age movement or conspiracy. It's not underground Satanism, psychic phenomena, or astrology. None of those dark forces are capable of propelling us into the end time. The force I'm talking about is simply this—the gospel going to all the world. Believe it or not, that's the most powerful force at work on our planet today. Jesus said to His followers, "This gospel of the kingdom shall be preached in all the world for a witness unto all nations; and then shall the end come" (Matthew 24:14).

The gospel will be preached all over the world, and then the end will come. That promise is echoed at the beginning of the message of the three angels in Revelation. The first messenger in Revelation 14:6 tells us that "the everlasting gospel" will be preached "to those who dwell on the earth—to every nation, tribe, tongue, and people." This prophecy is being fulfilled today. I have witnessed tens of thousands who have come to Christ in the former Communist countries. Over thirteen thousand people attended our meetings in Moscow's Kremlin

Palace. Red Army trucks delivered thirty thousand Bibles. In Moscow's Olympic Stadium, more than fifty thousand people attended our Christ-centered, Bible-based evangelistic meetings. The Spirit of God is on the move.

Recently, It Is Written Television signed a contract with a Hindu company in India with the potential of proclaiming the gospel to seventy-five million people in India. This station can reach 50 percent of the world's population via satellite. God is at work. Unusual things are happening.

In January of 1994, our Adventist World Radio began a powerful broadcast from two 250-kilowatt transmitters in the new republic of Slovakia. This new station broadcasts Christian programming twenty-four hours a day in Arabic, Czech, English, French, German, and India's four major languages. This means we are now covering all of central and eastern Africa, all of India, and all of the Middle East with the good news of Jesus Christ.

And then there's the newly built Adventist Media Center in Tula, Russia. Gospel radio programs in eight languages are distributed to five of the Russian government's most powerful transmitters. These programs, which are involving 65,000 people in Bible study, cover much of Europe and Asia, including China. Adventist World Radio programs like this now cover three-fourths of the world's population.

Yes, the good news is going out to billions. The signs of the times indicate that Jesus Christ *is* coming soon. His message *is* going to the ends of the earth. The gospel *is* being preached. Men and women *do* have an opportunity to hear the Word of God. This is no common time. This is no ordinary time. This is a time to open our hearts to Christ. This is a time to surrender our lives to Jesus. This is a time to prepare for His soon return.

It is not going to end with a bang. It is not going to end with a whimper. It is going to end with unimaginable terror and inexpressible joy. What will *you* feel during the last moments of earth's history? You can discover just how to experience life's happiest moment.

CHAPTER

THREE

The Last Minutes of History

The end will start out rather quietly—just a cloud, which looks about the size of a man's hand, appearing in the sky, coming from the direction of the constellation Orion. True enough, there'll be plenty of commotion on the ground. In fact, whole nations will be reeling from devastating plagues and deadly conflicts.

But, the last few moments of earth's history really begin with that small cloud. And the first thing human beings will feel is just curiosity.

Someone out on a ship at sea, scanning the horizon, will notice it: "What is that odd-looking cloud?" It appears rounder and brighter than the other clouds in the sky.

Someone watching for a plane to land will see it. Someone just staring at the heavens in a daydream will see it. At first, they'll just be curious: "What *is* that odd-looking cloud?"

But then, their eyes will widen. The cloud seems to be . . . yes, it's moving! It's growing bigger. It seems to be speeding toward planet Earth. Within moments, more and more people will look up at the sky. They're pointing. They're exclaiming.

It's more than curiosity they feel. It's a strange premonition. Something in the pit of their stomachs. People have seen unusual phenomena in the heavens before. They know about the northern lights, meteor showers, and streaking comets. But this is different. Could it be an alien spaceship? Could it be some secret military weapon?

The word spreads like wildfire. A young mother rocking her baby to sleep gets a call from her husband at the office. Has she heard? Has she seen it? The woman steps quickly to the living-room window and looks up. There it is. She clutches her child tightly to her breast.

School children in the playgrounds stop their games and stare. Construction workers drop their tools and look up. More and more people are rushing outside, emptying restaurants, theaters, and shopping malls.

The cloud keeps getting bigger and brighter and closer. People can't take their eyes off it.

What is it they're seeing? It's the fulfillment of a promise that Jesus Christ made. In Matthew 24:30, He told His followers what would happen right after the final disturbances of nature mark the end of time. "Then the sign of the Son of Man will appear in heaven, and then all the tribes of the earth . . . will see the Son of Man coming on the clouds of heaven with power and great glory" (Matthew 24:30, NKJV).

That cloud in the sky keeps getting bigger, because Jesus is returning to earth. This time He's coming not as a humble carpenter of Nazareth, not as a Galilean rabbi, but as King of kings and Lord of lords.

That cloud in the sky keeps getting brighter, because this time Christ is coming with power and great glory. And this time, every human being on the planet will witness His entry.

The apostle John reiterates the words of Matthew. "Behold, He is coming with clouds, and every eye will see Him" (Revelation 1:7, NKJV).

During those first few moments, as the cloud approaches the earth, more and more people stop what they're doing, more and more people lift up their faces, more and more people are transfixed by the sight—until all humanity is looking.

Jesus said His coming would be like lightning that comes from the east and flashes all the way across the heavens to the west, thus encircling the globe.

We get a little glimpse of what that's like during the Olympics, or the World Cup of soccer. Billions of people sit staring at their TV sets as these events come to them live, via satellite. It's as if the whole world is drawn into one communication system.

Well, the second coming of Christ is coming to us live, too, via Christ's own kind of satellite. He will project Himself around the world, and every individual will stare up into the heavens.

First, there will be just curiosity. Then a strange premonition. But, as the cloud approaches, people will catch their breath, pulses will quicken. Thousands of angels will materialize around the edges of the cloud, forming a dazzling pattern of white against the blue sky. And in the center of this swirl, Someone is there—still too brilliant to make out clearly.

A Decisive Moment

A decisive moment descends upon the residents of planet Earth.

As it becomes clear that God Himself is on His way to pay a visit, humanity divides itself into two distinct groups. Until that time, just about everyone has felt the same emotions of questioning, comprehension, and shock, but as the glory of the returning King floods over the world, some feel inexpressible joy—and others, unimaginable terror.

Some of the faces staring up at this new blazing sun in the heavens grow pale; some knees begin to tremble. People are horrified as they realize they've spent their lives running away from His holy presence. They've turned aside His appeals. They've ignored Him in a thousand different ways, and now it's too late to respond to His divine love.

Somewhere, a young man drops his briefcase and collapses on a sidewalk. He's been living life in the fast lane, sure that he'd make his first million before the age of 35. But now he realizes he's invested absolutely nothing in the one area of life that matters most. He hasn't given God the time of day since he was in Sunday School.

Some people will find the appearance of Jesus Christ in all His majesty to be a terrifying surprise, and they'll start running, trying to get away from the blinding light.

The apostle John saw this group's reaction in a vision. He recounts the reaction of these people in one of the most graphic, moving passages in all the Bible. They . . . "hid themselves in the caves and in the rocks of the mountains, and said to the mountains and rocks, 'Fall on us and hide us from the face of Him who sits on the throne and from the wrath of the Lamb! For the great day of His wrath has come, and who is able to stand?' " (Revelation 6:15-17, NKJV).

Guilty hearts make people afraid. Their own misdeeds accuse them, and they try to run away from God. But since there's really no place to hide, they hope the rocks will fall on them and crush out their lives. Overwhelming emotions cause them to be suicidal. Better to end it all than to face the King on His throne.

And their desperate prayers are answered. Scripture tells us the wicked are destroyed "with the brightness of His coming" (2 Thessalonians 2:8). Their unbearable terror ends in death.

This is what one group of people will experience during the final minutes of earth's history. But another group experiences something totally different.

A Joyous Moment

Somewhere, in front of a simple apartment building, a young woman grabs her little boy and lifts him up in her arms. "Look, Brian," she cries, "He's coming! It's really happening! Jesus is here!" This woman bears on her arms the scars of many years of drug abuse and in her heart the scars of too many broken relationships.

Yet, inside this woman is a faith that has been growing. In her hopelessness, she turned to the only One who seemed to care. She put her life in the hands of Jesus Christ. She accepted Him as her Saviour, and although she had little to give, she gave it all.

And now, there He is, above her in the sky, and in that instant, she knows she's been rescued—that eternity lies just moments away. She begins to think about what life in heaven will be like, and the joy is too much. Tears flow down her cheeks.

Somewhere walking along the beach, an elderly couple cling

to each other, looking up. They try to speak, but they can't; they just keep shaking their heads in wonder. Nevertheless, they feel the unspoken bond of the faith they share. It's brought them through a lot—times of financial hardship and sickness, times when their children renounced their faith, times of sickness and disappointment.

Some tragedies even seemed to obliterate God's face, but they held strong to their faith. They trusted the Lord. They kept their lives in His hands.

And now, finally, the day of glory is here, bursting out of the sky all around them. And their joy makes all their troubles seem light and momentary.

As the apostle Peter wrote of believers receiving salvation, he described them as being rejoicing "with joy inexpressible and full of glory" (1 Peter 1:8).

The woman and couple are part of a group of people who are eager to meet God. They know they're weak and sinful, but they also know they're forgiven. They know they're accepted by the grace of Jesus Christ.

Thousands of years ago, the prophet Isaiah looked forward to this great event and, in hopeful, encouraging words, described the emotions of sincere believers who will look up and see Jesus when He comes: "And it will be said in that day: 'Behold, this is our God; we have waited for Him, and He will save us. This is the Lord; we have waited for Him; we will be glad and rejoice in His salvation' " (Isaiah 25:9 NKJV).

They've been waiting so long. And now, at last, the event they've yearned for is upon them as their loving Saviour approaches earth. Just as believers think they have attained maximum joy, something else happens—something very wonderful.

Somewhere, in a small family cemetery on the wind-swept prairie, the earth breaks open. The flowers that a grieving mother has placed by the tombstone are thrust aside. A tiny coffin opens up, and a baby's voice cries out. Instantly, an angel darts from the sky and gathers the infant into his arms. In another instant, he's beside the mother, who's been gazing in stunned silence at the heavens.

The mother stares at her child for a second. The last time she looked at that tiny face, it was pale and full of pain, losing a battle against a deadly disease. But now, the child is cooing; his flesh is warm and pink again; his eyes bright as he looks into his mother's face. And trembling, the woman takes the baby to her and holds him close. When she turns to thank the angel, he's already flown off on another mission.

Somewhere, in a city cemetery, a young couple finds themselves standing beside their own open graves. At first, they're completely disoriented in the bright light around them. They have no idea how they got there. The last thing they remember is a tractor-trailer heading straight toward them on the highway. Did they somehow survive the accident? They notice their names on the tombstones, look up, and catch their breaths. The man and woman reach for each other as they stare at the heavens.

This is it! This is Jesus Christ appearing. This is the One to whom they dedicated themselves, and now the whole planet is lighted up with His presence. Now they know they'll never, ever be parted again. They'll have an eternity to grow in their love.

In the last few minutes of earth's history, the planet will be shaken with countless resurrections. And everywhere you'll hear the cries of recognition; loved ones who have been torn apart by tragedy will fall into each other's arms.

Glorious Reunion

Believers begin to notice that their feet are no longer on the ground. They suddenly feel weightless. They've started to rise up to meet the spectacle in the heavens. Many of the joyful reunions, in fact, happen in midair—families embracing on their way to meet Jesus.

And now the face of the Saviour really is coming close. It seems to fill the whole sky. The joyful voices of believers rise up to meet the trumpet sound and the call of angels echoing down from the cloud.

The moment that Paul anticipated has arrived! "The Lord Himself will descend from heaven with a shout, with the voice of an archangel, and with the trumpet of God. And the dead in Christ will rise first. Then we who are alive and remain shall be caught up together with them in the clouds to meet the Lord in the air. And thus we shall always be with the Lord" (1 Thessalonians 4:16, 17, NKJV).

Rising up to meet the Lord of lords, the Prince of Peace, the Wonderful Counselor, the Good Shepherd. Rising up to meet the Creator of all life in the universe. Rising up to meet an eternal destiny with Jesus. What inexpressible joy!

Believers will have to be radically changed in order to contain it all. They will be changed, as Scripture says, in the twinkling of an eye. Mortal human flesh takes on immortality; weak and broken minds and bodies are remade, perfectly whole.

The ultimate reunion with Jesus Christ takes place just above the surface of the earth. These are the last moments, the last seconds of human history. This is where eternity begins for faithful believers.

Your Choice

Think about that glorious reunion as you ponder this. Where will you be during the last minutes of earth's history? What will you be experiencing? What will you be feeling? Will it be unimaginable terror—or inexpressible joy? You may feel rather indifferent about God right now. You may not think faith is so important. But one day soon, it will make all the difference in the world. One day soon, it will divide humanity into two groups for all eternity.

One group will experience the second coming of Christ as a horrifying surprise. The other will experience it as a wonderful deliverance, as a fulfillment of all they've lived for. One group will be praying for the rocks to fall on them. The other will be shouting ecstatically, "This is our God, we've waited for Him."

Please don't put off an encounter with Jesus Christ until it's too late. Please don't wait until you see Him bursting through the heavens. Make a commitment to Jesus today. Open up your heart today; ask Jesus right now if there is anything in your life that stands between you and Him.

Many of the leading thinkers of this world recognize that our world is on the verge of a stupendous crisis. They sense that we're living in the last minutes of earth's history. But there is hope for our confused, chaotic planet. There is hope for our overpopulated, polluted world. There is hope for our crime-riddled streets. There is hope for our broken hearts and broken families. Jesus' promise is still true. He says, "I will come again."

And when He comes, you can look up and meet Him in joy. You can look up and meet Him in gladness and happiness.

> Do you have an inner love hunger, a longing for love that won't be quenched? Let yourself be embraced by the love of God now, so that you can be secure in His arms when He comes. As you read this chapter, you will discover His love anew, today, so you can meet Him in peace tomorrow.

CHAPTER

FOUR

Embraced by Love at End Time

Kim was excited! Maybe excited is too mild a word. She was euphoric! She was wild with delight. Her husband, Steve, had just won the Ohio state lottery of several million dollars—$107,000 per year for twenty years. To top it off, he won the lottery a second time to the tune of $100,000. This Dayton couple could live the life of their dreams. Incredible pleasures lay at their fingertips.

There was only one problem. Kim was having an extramarital affair, and she knew the win would only cause greater problems. She didn't want to walk away from millions but certainly didn't want to end the affair either. She wanted Steve's money but had no interest in him.

The lottery winnings dominated Kim's mind. Passionately, she plotted to get the money and finally came up with a plan to hire a hit man to assassinate her husband.

While she discussed her plan on the phone with her lover, her twenty-one-year-old son was listening to the entire conversation. The young man informed his dad, who immediately contacted the police. Kim was arrested for plotting her husband's death for a mere $500. She had put $25 down, with the balance to be paid when the job was done.

Surprisingly enough, Steve repeatedly visited Kim in prison. "You don't wash twenty-two years under the bridge," he explained. Their relationship grew. He diligently fought to have her sentence reduced. He dropped all charges against her. Ultimately, he bailed her out. His love broke her heart. His loving initiative touched something deep inside. Kim saw her affair for what it was—a cheap imitation of the real thing. How could she resist the real, genuine, authentic love of one who would not let her go? How could she be unfaithful to somebody so faithful to her? How could she turn her back on one who embraced her with his love? She couldn't. She wouldn't. When he bailed her out of prison, she threw her arms around him sobbing, "Please, never, never, never let me go!"

Their friends call them crazy, and Steve and Kim don't disagree. "Love is a state of insanity anyway," Steve said. "You just cannot explain it."

Unexplainable Love

Is there anyone who loves you that much? Do you mean so much to someone that even if you cheated on them and plotted to kill them, they would lovingly embrace you? You may not realize it, but there is One who loves you that much. There is One who cares for you that much. There is One who will never let you go.

Come with me to a garden—the powder blue cloudless

sky and warm summer rays speak of another day in Eden. The earth is carpeted with a velvetlike grass covering. Birds sing their happy songs. Flowers dot the landscape. The lion and lamb play together. There is no worry, fear, anxiety, or tension. The atmosphere is charged with love. A gentle calm settles over the landscape. This inner peace, combined with a zest for living, energizes Adam and Eve. Eden is heaven on earth. Everything our first parents need or can possibly desire is present. They have no unfulfilled needs. There is no restless longing for something they don't have. They are completely satisfied. Fellowship with God and one another in their Eden home brings an unexplainable joy.

When an intruder enters, all this changes. Doubt replaces confidence. Suspicion overshadows trust. Conflict pushes peace aside. Selfishness strangles love. The evil one claims that God is holding out on them. Satan insinuates that God does not have their greatest good in view. Urging them to disobey, he promises an exhilarating freedom. The Scriptures describe the drama this way:

> The serpent said unto the woman, Ye shall not surely die: For God doth know that in the day ye eat thereof, then your eyes shall be opened, and ye shall be as gods, knowing good and evil. And when the woman saw that the tree was good for food, and that it was pleasant to the eyes, and a tree to be desired to make one wise, she took of the fruit thereof, and did eat, and gave also unto her husband with her; and he did eat" (Genesis 3:4-6).

Charmed by another lover, Eve fell for his seductive lies. In a mad dash for pleasure, she yielded. His voice was soft and sweet, his offer enticing. Maybe God didn't have her best interest in mind. Maybe His laws were hard and restrictive. Possibly this "other lover's" offer was much more gratifying. Was she missing something? Something this illicit relationship could provide? The decision was made. The act performed. The forbidden fruit eaten.

Her pleasure was short-lived. Shame followed quickly on the heels of ecstasy. Guilt like a cancer gnawed away at her insides. Joy danced away like grains of sand slipping through her fingers. Confusion clouded her mind. She had sinned, and she knew it. There was no excuse! Now she was trapped . . . destined for death. God's words, "In the day that thou eatest thereof thou shalt surely die" (Genesis 2:17) echoed and reechoed in her mind. Sin is separation from God (see Isaiah 59:1, 2). God is the source of happiness, joy, and life for the universe (see John 10:10; 14:6). Severed from His life-giving love, Eve died spiritually that day. She also died emotionally and began to die physically. Life would never be the same again. Her affair with the evil one changed her forever. She left the One who really loved her. She yielded to the one who only intended to selfishly abuse her. She squandered a fortune to receive a pittance. She spurned the affections of One who truly loved her to embrace one who would only destroy her. Shackled in the chains of her own sin, she had little hope. Imprisoned by her ill choice, she was left broken by the evil one. She tempted her spouse, who also succumbed.

Forgiveness

Guilt-ridden, they tried to hide but heard the footsteps of God in the garden. Gently, kindly, lovingly His voice called, "Adam, Eve, where are you?" God took the initiative. He came looking for the estranged couple. There in the garden, God gave them reason to hope again. He honestly explained the result of their sin—heartache, sorrow, disappointment. Broken hearts and broken homes, weariness and worry, bombs and battles, disease and death. But beyond their bondage, love would break through. The Messiah would come.

This planet in rebellion would be visited by love. God would enter into human flesh. Jesus would reveal what God is like. Every time He opened blind eyes, He declared, God is like that. Each time He fed the hungry, He said God is like that. When He raised the dead, He revealed that God desires us to live, not die.

When He forgave those who nailed Him to a wooden cross, He declared "God is like that! He, too, forgives." When He delivered the demoniacs, he triumphantly shouted, "God is like that—no power in hell can hold you down!"

Come with me now to a dusty, rutted hill and a windswept knoll spotted with blood—Golgotha by name. Watch as Jesus stumbles three times beneath the load. The heavy cross crushes His shoulders. Watch as cruel Roman soldiers violently stretch out His arms. Behold as they drive crude, jagged nails through His wrists. Listen to the thud of the cross as it is thrust into a hole. Listen to His words, "Father, forgive them, for they do not know what they do" (Luke 23:34, NKJV). While blood oozed from His palms and spurted from His side, forgiveness flowed from His heart.

The cross speaks of God's unmatchable love and His unending mercy. On the cross, Jesus willingly carried the guilt of our sins. Since the wages of sin is death (Romans 6:23), if Christ had not assumed the responsibility for our sins, we would have to accept the consequences of our own sins—eternal death. He never sinned, but He became sin for us (2 Corinthians 8:21).

When we by faith accept Christ, we accept His death in our behalf. We exclaim with the apostle Paul, "He loved me and died for me" (see Galatians 2:20). As we meditate upon the cross, we realize that our sins nailed Jesus there. We deserve to die, but the perfect, spotless Son of God dies in our place. By faith we accept His death in the place of our own death. Nothing we can do on our own is adequate to earn our salvation. We are saved solely by His grace (Ephesians 2:8). As we "confess our sins, He is faithful and just to forgive us our sins, and to cleanse us from all unrighteousness" (1 John 1:9).

Acceptance

God accepts us as His children, and when we understand this, the guilt is gone. There is no condemnation for those who are in Christ Jesus (Romans 8:1). His righteous life becomes ours by faith. We appear before God as if we had never sinned. We stand perfect in His sight through Jesus Christ. His love is a redeeming love, a saving love, a reconciling love. His love entered into the depths of death itself to save us. Jesus was willing to risk eternal loss Himself, to be eternally separated from the Father, to redeem us. When He cried, "My God, My God, why hast thou forsaken Me," He feared that His separation from God might be eternal. He sensed that a judgment bar was set up on Calvary. Christ was judged a sinner on our behalf. He endured the same agony, the same separation from God, that sinners will feel when they experience eternal loss. He entered the depths of hell so we could rise to the heights of heaven. He died the death that was ours, so we could live the life that was His.

In Revelation, the Bible's last book, the apostle John describes the dramatic scenes of heaven's final judgment. The destiny of the entire race will be settled forever. This cosmic judgment proceeds directly from the throne of God. All heaven is hushed. Angelic beings look upon the scene with intense interest. An angel eagerly inquires, "Who is worthy to open the book, and to loose the seals thereof?" (Revelation 5:2). In other words, who is righteous enough to appear before a holy God? Who can stand for faulty, guilty, condemned sinners in the judgment? Heaven breaks into weeping. No one in heaven or earth is pure enough, holy enough, righteous enough. At this decisive moment, a heavenly being steps forth. In tenderest compassion He says, "Stop crying, don't weep anymore." Jesus, pictured as the Lamb of God, bruised and bleeding, steps forward (verse 6).

Why does the apostle picture a bleeding lamb in heaven? Jesus was our Saviour on earth, and He is still our Saviour in heaven. He redeemed us on the cross of Calvary. He met the claims of a broken law head-on. He bore all the condemnation of our sin in His body. Jesus, the bruised, bloody, battered Lamb who died for us now represents us before heaven's final judgment. He presents His spotless, righteous, sinless life on our behalf.

As I look at myself with all my faults and imperfections, my sins and weaknesses, there is no possibility I can be saved. When I look at Jesus with all His righteousness and holiness, all His obedience and perfection, there is no possibility I can be lost. Accepting Him, I accept His righteousness, His holiness, His perfection. He willingly took all my guilt, shame, and condemnation with Him to the cross.

Now He presents me before His Father in heaven's final judgment, just as if I had never sinned . . . just as if I had lived perfectly all the time. What incredible love! What amazing compassion! What infinite mercy!

Love That Goes the Distance

On December 31, 1995, John Clancy, veteran firefighter in New York City, led his crew into a burning vacant apartment building in a lower Manhattan drug district. As the fire raged out of control, the firefighters were concerned that someone might still be in the apartment building, although the only ones who used it were vagrants, drug addicts, alcoholics, and prostitutes. Nevertheless, Clancy and his colleagues decided to enter the blazing inferno to conduct a search and rescue operation. The building was filled with smoke, making visibility almost zero. The firefighters were risking their lives to find vagrants who might be using the building as a temporary home.

Suddenly the second-floor ceiling collapsed, trapping John Clancy. His colleagues worked feverishly to deliver him from the fiery holocaust, but when they finally pulled him out, it was too late. His body was burned beyond recognition. The last day of 1995 was the last day of this courageous firefighter's life. He left behind a wife who was six months pregnant and the future they were planning together.

John Clancy believed that all life was valuable; therefore, he was willing to risk his own to save whoever might be in the building. He left the safety of his own home for the danger of a raging fire. He entered the flames to save lives and lost his own. His devotion to duty cost him his life. He could not stand idly by when he knew others were dying.

As details of this story were uncovered, investigators discovered that the fire had been caused by arson. Edwin Smith, one of the "down and outers" who was reportedly in the building, set the fire. The hard fact is, John Clancy was attempting to save the one who burned the building down. He gave his life for an arsonist.

As Billy Graham so aptly put it, "Ours is a world aflame." When Adam and Eve sinned, they lighted a match that set the tinder of this world ablaze. The fires of sin engulfed the planet. Unbridled passion, uncontrolled anger, the fires of a thousand sins all raged out of control. Death was the inevitable result. There was no way out.

At the crisis hour, Jesus leapt into the flames. He saw this planet as a raging inferno destined for disaster. He knew we were doomed to death. The Saviour gave His life for "spiritual arsons." We started the fire with the sparks of our own sins.

The Old Testament presents a graphic picture of Christ the Deliverer in the book of Daniel. Daniel's friends, Shadrach, Meshach, and Abednego, were cast into Nebuchadnezzar's fiery furnace. They, too, were destined for death. When the king gazed into the flames, he saw four men alive, the fourth being Jesus, the mighty Deliverer. He stood in the midst of the flames to deliver the three Hebrew worthies from certain death. Without Him, there was no hope. With Him, there was no impossible situation.

At the end of time, our world will be a burning inferno. Our God is a consuming fire to sin wherever it is found (Hebrews 12:29). When Christ returns, the wicked will be destroyed by His flaming presence (2 Thessalonians 1:8). They will be consumed—burned to ashes—gone forever (Malachi 3:1-4). Out of the ashes of this old world God will create a new world (2 Peter 3:10-13).

If you have not yet accepted Christ as your Saviour, He desires to save you today. He desires to leap into the flames of your life, to touch you with His love, to pardon your sins, to forgive your guilty past, and to transform your life. The flames of sin today need not overcome you. The fiery presence of God, which will purify the earth, need not destroy you along with sin. You can come to Jesus today. Your sins can be pardoned today. You can receive His mercy today. He gave His life for you. He suffered the agony of hell itself for you. What more could love give? Come to Him today and experience the joy of being embraced by His love.

Why not pray this prayer right now—

> Jesus, I thank You for Your love. I know that I have sinned. There is nothing I can do to earn eternal life. I don't deserve it. I thank You that You freely offer it to me just now. I praise You for leaping into the flames, for taking my penalty in Your own body, for experiencing the agony of hell itself for me.
>
> Just now I accept Your sacrifice in my behalf. Thank You for such incredible love. I confess my sins and accept Your forgiveness, believing I have the gift of eternal life through Jesus Christ, my Lord. Amen.

Have you every wondered how to overcome undesirable habits? Why is it that we stumble and fall again and again? What is the essence of true religion? You can experience Christ's life-changing power today to prepare you for His coming tomorrow.

CHAPTER
FIVE

Ready for His Return

It was a new day. For once I had arrived at Heathrow Airport early. It was August 1, 1990. My wife and I had just completed five delightful years serving Christ in Europe. Our flight was scheduled to leave at 6:30 p.m. We had arrived at the airport around 3:45 p.m. But upon arriving at the check-in gate, I was dismayed to learn that our plane was three hours late. This meant a whopping six-hour wait in the airport. I despise waiting in airports. What would we do for the next six hours?

We checked our bags through and waited. We waited and then waited some more. We ate and talked. We read and ate again. And finally, we walked down to the gate around 8:00 o'clock, only to learn that there would be still another delay. By now we were restless, super anxious to get home. Soon ours was the only flight left on the schedule board—all the others had left. It was approaching midnight. The airport was closing down. Many passengers were sprawled out on the chairs, sleeping. Those of us who managed to stay awake were drowsy. Suddenly an announcement was made. "Flight 701 for New York City, LaGuardia Airport, is now ready for boarding."

People began to stir. Quickly they gathered their belongings. Half asleep, my wife Teenie and I jumped up. She spoke first. "Let's go. We're going home!" As we rushed toward the boarding gate, one lone traveler attracted our attention. She was sleeping through it all and would surely miss her flight. Someone needed to have the courage to wake her up. My wife went over and shook her and graciously asked, "Are you headed for New York?" Wiping her eyes, she nodded. "The flight's boarding." She nodded in the affirmative. My wife then added, "The flight is boarding, it's time to get on. Let's go."

"Oh, thank you for waking me up," the young woman replied. "I'm certain I would have missed my flight."

A Parable of Our Time

What a parable of our time. Many professed Christians say they are waiting for the coming of Jesus. But their lives indicate that they are asleep. Their actions reveal that their hearts are somewhere else.

In Jesus' parable of the ten virgins, He discusses a delay of the coming of the bridegroom. The wedding party anticipated that the ceremony would take place much sooner. When it didn't occur as expected, they, too, slept. At midnight, the darkest hour, the announcement was made. "Behold, the bridegroom is coming; go out to meet him!" (Matthew 25:6, NKJV). In the parable, half of the bridesmaids were ready, the other half were not. Half of them were prepared, the other half were surprised. Half of them were saved, the other half were lost. They all were waiting for the coming of the bridegroom. They all anticipated that He was coming. They all had an invitation to be ready, yet half of them were unprepared. Why?

What does it mean to be ready for the coming of Christ? Is it more than mere profession? Is it more than simple desire? Is it more than talking about being ready?

Mahatma Gandhi once stated that if Christians lived like the Christ they professed, all India would become Christian. In many Christian circles today, there is a lot of talk about Christ, with little action for Him. There's a great deal of emphasis on externals but not much on devotion. Heart religion, Christ in the life, God's law written on the inside—that's the kind of faith that will prepare us for the second coming of Christ. To be ready for the second coming means that we accept Him first as our Saviour and Lord. We will never be able to worship Him as the King of the universe, unless we have first accepted Him as King of our heart.

Jesus reserved some of His most scathing rebukes for the professed religious people of His day. The Pharisees fasted, prayed, and gave significant offerings. They memorized Scripture. They meticulously observed the Sabbath. They followed the laws of health. These devout Hebrews emphasized obligation. But for many, religion became a burdensome requirement. Something totally separate from what took place in the heart.

And Jesus stated it clearly when He said, "We've got to find a righteousness that surpasses that of the Pharisees." He became quite specific about what His religion of the heart would do. If love fills us instead of anger—if generosity wells up inside instead of selfishness; if a longing for righteousness consumes us instead of a longing for possessions, then amazing things will start to happen.

In the Sermon on the Mount, Jesus actually suggested that if a bad-tempered person strikes you on the right cheek, turn to him the left. He continued, "If someone wants your tunic, offer him your cloak as well. If a Roman soldier forces you to carry his pack one mile, disarm him, carry it two miles." Jesus' words about loving one's enemies must have been the hardest for those people on that Galilean hillside to take. It's easy to love your friends. A converted heart shows love for one's enemies.

Jesus: Our Saviour

A true follower of Christ is one who has accepted Jesus as Saviour. His blood shed on Calvary redeems us. His grace pardons us. His extended mercy provides salvation. The ground of our salvation is Jesus Christ. The foundation of our salvation is the cross of Calvary. We are not saved by our works. To act as though we are saved by works is to deny Christ as our Saviour. Salvation is a gift full and complete in Christ (see Ephesians 2:8; Romans 3:20-24; 6:23).

Jesus: Our Lord

The same faith that accepts Him as Saviour receives Him as Lord. A genuine disciple of Christ is one who has surrendered to the lordship of Christ. Jesus is the ideal example of the fully-surrendered life. Come with me to a garden called Gethsemane. The fate of the world trembles in the balance. Jesus bows low beneath the ancient olive trees and pours out His life. Before Him are the crown of thorns, the spear, and the nails. In a few hours He will be tried in Pilate's judgment hall. His back will be lacerated, with hunks of flesh ripped out by the Roman lash. Jesus will suffer in agony. Calvary's hill and

Golgotha's mountain lie before Him. His humanity shrinks from the cross. If possible, He longs to avoid it. But here, in Gethsemane, with His face buried in the warm earth, in the darkness of night, beneath the starry heavens, Jesus cries out, "O My Father, if it is possible, let this cup [of suffering] pass from Me; nevertheless, not as I will, but as You will" (Matthew 26:39, NKJV). When we accept Christ as Lord of our life, we will trust Him, just as He trusted His Father, no matter where He leads. We will be able to say, as He did, "Not my will, but Thy will be done."

His Surrendered Will

Jesus had a will of His own. But His will was surrendered to the higher will of His Father. Jesus' life commitment was to do the will of the Father. He states it clearly in John 8:29. "He that sent me is with me: the Father hath not left me alone; for I do always those things that please him." Jesus' passionate desire was to please the Father. His single-minded objective was to do God's will. When His human will pulled in one direction, He chose to surrender His desires for the Father's wishes. The psalmist, speaking prophetically of Jesus, declared, "I delight to do thy will, O my God: yea, thy law is within my heart" (Psalm 40:8).

The Holy Spirit leads us to Jesus and places a desire to do right in our hearts. When we yield to the Spirit's prompting and surrender to the convictions of the Holy Spirit, God gives us the power to carry out our choice. When we surrender our will to God's, He promises to do for us what we could never accomplish for ourselves. The choice is ours. The power to carry it out is His. Even if you have been a Christian all your life, apparently making right choices, it is God who has been working to lead you to make those choices.

The work from the beginning to the end of the Christian life is God's. God took the initiative in sending Christ to die for us. God takes the initiative in sending the Holy Spirit to draw us to Himself. God creates within us the desire to serve Him. God gives us the power to live the Christian life. But there is one thing God cannot and will not do. God will not make the choice for us. God will not coerce us or force us to surrender our will to His. In the final conflict between the forces of good and evil, God graciously grants us the power of choice. All of hell's mighty powers cannot force us to do wrong. All of heaven's superior powers will not coerce us to do right.

Searching for Chewing Tobacco

Bill, a friend of mine, told me a story about his father. Years ago, the family lived on a farm. Bill's dad was chewing tobacco and trying to quit. Early in the morning, Bill would see his dad walking back and forth in front of the little farmhouse fighting a terrible craving to chew tobacco. Pacing back and forth, he chose to quit. The old man took his chewing tobacco in his hand and threw it far out into the cornfield. Now he was free. He was done chewing tobacco.

But, as Bill tells the story, along about noon, he would see his dad out there among the corn stalks, head bent low, looking for something. What was he searching for? The tobacco that he had thrown out in the morning!

Here's my question. If you were God, would you let him find it? "Oh no!" somebody says. "God would not let him find it!" But God did. Why? Because He gave Bill's dad the same power of choice in the afternoon that He did in the morning. God does not manipulate the will.

God allows us to make choices. When we choose to put our will on the side of right, the Holy Spirit enters into our life. When that choice is genuine, we long to give up sin. When we surrender that specific habit and open our hearts to God, the Lord Himself comes into our lives in remarkable, dramatic ways.

The apostle declares, "I will put my laws into their hearts, and in their minds will I write them" (Hebrews 10:16). Paul makes it clear in 2 Corinthians 5:17 when he says, "If any man be in Christ, he is a new creature." Most modern translations say "he is a new creation." The work of creation occurs all over again. Just as at Creation Christ spoke and a world was created, He speaks again through the power of His Holy Spirit, and a new heart is created within us. At Creation, God created something out of nothing. In the new creation, God takes our pride, jealousy, dishonesty, anger, and immoral thoughts, and creates the fruits of the Spirit in our lives. Where there was hatred, there is now love. Where there was anger, there is now peace. Where there was depression, there is now joy. Where there was lust, there is now self-control. Where there was arrogance, there is now meekness.

The greatest evidence that we are Christians is a changed life. Our thought patterns are different. The focus of our attention is different. Our conversation is different. The center of our life is no longer what pleases us. It is now what pleases Him. Christ gives us new strength to do His will. We are changed. The greatest desire of our life is to do His will.

The Desire to Obey Him

When you are in love, you desire to please the one you love. Christianity is not merely something to believe, it is Someone to love. When we sense the depth of Christ's love for us, it breaks our hard, selfish heart. We long to please Him. Obeying Him becomes life's greatest joy.

Two thousand years ago, Jesus stated it clearly. "If ye love me, keep my commandments" (John 14:15). Love for God always leads to obedience. In the last days of earth's history, God will have a people who love Him so deeply that they long to obey Him. The last book of the Bible, Revelation, describes their last-day obedience in these words,

> "Here is the patience of the saints: Here are they that keep the commandments of God, and the faith of Jesus" (Revelation 14:12).

Doing the will of God is a hallmark of God's last-day people. Loving Christ is not merely pious sentimentalism, it is a matter of doing God's will. Christ's words are too plain to be misunderstood:

> Not every one that saith unto me, Lord, Lord, shall enter into the kingdom of heaven; but he that doeth the will of my Father which is in heaven.
>
> Many will say to me in that day, Lord, Lord, have we not prophesied in thy name? and in thy name have cast out devils? and in thy name done many wonderful works? And then will I profess unto them, I never knew you: depart from me, ye that work iniquity (Matthew 7:21-23).

A mere profession of Christ will not save you. A superficial, shallow Christianity will not get you through the days ahead. Jesus' words are clear. Last-day religion must be a religion that loves Christ so deeply it leads to a transformed life—a life of obedience.

The Story of a Modern-day Disciple

Richard Wurmbrand, a valiant soldier of the cross in Communist lands, watched God transform the most difficult lives.

Late one evening, three men conversed in a small flat in Budapest—Wurmbrand, who was a Lutheran pastor, his landlord, and Borila, a huge soldier on leave from the front where the Rumanians were fighting as allies with the Germans during World War II.

Borila dominated the conversation, boasting of his adventures in battle and especially of how he had volunteered to help exterminate Jews in Transmistria and had killed hundreds with his own hands.

Wurmbrand realized with horror that his own wife's family had been murdered in the same place. This man bragging before him may well have been the killer. The pastor was filled with indignation. But as they continued talking, something else began to fill his heart. Wurmbrand himself had been converted from a life of immorality when he read the life of Christ in the Gospels. Christ's teachings had overwhelmed him. And one of those teachings was to love your enemies. Wurmbrand began to see in this cruel man someone Jesus was trying to reach. He invited him down to his apartment to hear some of the Ukrainian melodies that the soldier said he liked so much.

Wurmbrand began playing the piano—softly so as not to awaken his wife and baby son. After a little while he could see the soldier was moved by the music. He stopped playing and said, "If you look through that curtain, you can see someone asleep in the next room. It's my wife, Sabina. Her parents, her sisters, and her twelve-year-old brother were killed with the rest of the family. You told me that you killed hundreds of Jews near Golta, and that's where they were taken. You yourself don't know who you shot, so we can assume that you are the murderer of her family."

Borila leaped from his chair, his eyes ablaze, looking as if he could strangle the pastor. But Wurmbrand calmed him by proposing an experiment: "I'll wake up my wife and tell her who you are, and what you've done. And I can tell you what will happen. My wife will not speak one word of reproach. She'll embrace you as if you were her brother. She'll bring you supper, the best things she has in the house."

The pastor then came to the punch line: "If Sabina, who is a sinner like us, can forgive you and love you like this, imagine how Jesus, who is so perfect, can forgive and love you!" He urged Borila to return to God and seek forgiveness.

The man melted. Rocking back and forth, he sobbed out his confession: "I'm a murderer; I'm a murderer; I'm soaked in blood." Wurmbrand guided him to his knees and began praying. Borila begged for forgiveness over and over again. He asked God to give him new desires. He asked God to give him a new heart. He was willing to surrender, but he needed the power of God in his life.

When they were finished praying, the pastor walked into his bedroom and gently awakened his wife. "There's a man here whom you must meet," he whispered. "We believe he has murdered your family, but he has repented, and now he's our brother. He, too, is a disciple of Christ."

Sabina came out in her dressing gown and extended her hands to the huge, tear-stained soldier. He collapsed in her arms, and they wept bitterly. Finally Sabina went into the kitchen to prepare some food.

Wurmbrand thought that his guest could use a further

reinforcement of grace, so he stepped into the next room and returned with his two-year-old son, Mihai, fast asleep in his arms. Borila was dismayed. It had only been hours since he had boasted of killing Jewish children in their parents' arms, now this sight seemed an unbearable reproach. He expected a withering rebuke from his host.

Instead, the pastor leaned forward and said, "Do you see how quietly he sleeps? You are like a newborn child who can rest in the Father's arms. As you surrendered your life to Christ, His Spirit is working inside you to help you grow just like my son will grow. The blood that Jesus has shed has cleansed you. His Spirit working inside you will enable you to continue to reveal what He is like.

Looking down at Mihai, Borila felt, for the first time in ages, a surge of pure happiness.

When Borila rejoined his regiment in Russia, he laid aside his weapons and volunteered to rescue the wounded under fire. The law of God had been written in his heart. He had surrendered his will to Christ. He received Christ's forgiveness and His life-changing power. He became a genuine follower of Christ. He lived a life of loving obedience to the Christ who saved him.

Have you opened your heart to this Christ? Have you responded to the claims of His Spirit? Have you surrendered to His will? Do you desire to be ready for His return? Allow His love to break your heart. Borila's life was dramatically changed. Yours can be too! You can be a new you. Your one desire can be to please Him. When Christ comes, He will come for those who have the all-consuming desire to please Him. For when you are really in love, it shows— not in words alone but in deeds.

Does your prayer life seem boring? At times do your prayers seem to go no higher than the ceiling? Do you wonder, Is there Somebody out there listening? Or am I just praying to myself? You can fellowship with God today in preparation for seeing Him face to face tomorrow.

CHAPTER

SIX

The Stuff of Survival

On the five-hundredth anniversary of Columbus' finding the New World, NASA launched a new age of discovery. At precisely 3:00 p.m., October 12, 1992, an astronomer in Puerto Rico started the biggest radio telescope on earth on a quest for life beyond our planet. This aluminum bowl, 1,000 feet across, suspended over a deep gorge, began to search for evidence of advanced civilizations elsewhere in the Milky Way as part of Project SETI, the Search for Extra Terrestrial Intelligence.

At the same moment, another scientist in the Mojave Desert turned on a Goldstone Tracking Station radio telescope. These two dishes working together began tuning their electronic ears for something different from the background noise of the universe, some telling signal that says, "Here we are. Let's talk."

It's an enormous project, requiring four million dollars per year in private funding since Congress cut SETI funds out of NASA's budget in 1993. Radio telescopes are zeroing in on frequencies at the microwave end of the spectrum. These are the "quiet channels" of space that have the least interference. Scientists are guessing that extraterrestrials trying to communicate across the galaxies will be smart enough to broadcast on these frequencies. After all, it's the only way to be heard above the cosmic background noise of the stars.

What is behind this huge project? Just one thing: the hope of hearing a voice talk back to us, the hope of an intelligent echo somewhere in this vast universe. All this complex assortment of high technology is focusing on space just for the chance of hearing a voice in the dark.

Yet, with our electronic ears straining so hard to hear some faint ping-ping from space, many of us may be missing the most important extraterrestrial voice of all. We may have grown deaf to the most intelligent signals ever beamed our way.

The Most Important Message of All

Jeremiah the prophet speaks with relevance to this generation. He says: "Thus says the LORD who made it, the LORD who formed it to establish it . . . 'Call to Me, and I will answer you, and show you great and mighty things, which you do not know' " (Jeremiah 33:2, 3, NKJV). Long before anyone had ever dreamed up the radio telescope, Jeremiah assured his contemporaries that the Creator was very much on the line, ready to communicate, ready to enlighten us with His wisdom.

The irony is, that while we expend millions on the remote chance of a stray call from ET, we ignore the "still, small voice" whispering in our ear. The Creator of the Universe wants to talk, but we're too busy sorting through the cosmic background noise. We're straining to catch a flicker of intelligence somewhere out in space, but we ignore the LORD who knocks on the doors of our hearts.

Why is it that prayer doesn't seem nearly as exciting as receiving signals from space? Why is it that talking to God by faith doesn't seem as full of potential as checking radio frequencies by telescope? The Almighty actually assures us that through prayer we can get to know Him intimately, that we can have a face-to-face encounter. Listen to this promise given in Psalm 145:18: "The Lord is near to all who call upon Him, to all who call upon Him in truth" (Psalm 145:18, NKJV).

God comes close to all who call on Him. That's the promise. That's the incredible potential of prayer. And yet for most people, it feels more like a shot in the dark. God's face doesn't seem to come close when they pray. They don't experience a satisfying sense of intimacy.

Why? Why do so many fail to come up with any signs of celestial intelligence when they tune in the divine frequency? Why do prayers fall flat so often?

Let me share one very important reason with you. Often we come to God earnestly only when emergencies strike. A lot of people end up like the irreligious sailor who, as his ship was tossed about in the sea, cried out, "O Lord, I've not asked You for anything for the last fifteen years, and if You deliver us out of this storm, I promise, God, I'll not bother You for another fifteen years."

It's a good idea, of course, to pray when calamity strikes. The problem is, when things are going OK, we tend to pray vaguely, if at all; when things go haywire, we pray specifically. If dropping to our knees is just a way to dodge some blow, then we're really missing out on the best part of prayer.

Prayer Is About Communication

As the verses we read point out, prayer is about communication; it's about understanding the mind and the heart of God. That takes time; that requires an ongoing dialogue.

Ask yourself this question: how much quality time have I spent with God? If prayer is just an occasional cry for help, then we're not that different from those astronomers scanning the vast heavens for some sign of intelligence. They hope that with a bit of luck, they might hit on something.

Many people are calling out to a God in the distance, a God up there somewhere. And they wonder if anybody is really listening. After all, what are the chances of this little speck of humanity in this corner of space ever getting a message through to the nerve center of the universe?

Trying to reach ET is truly a shot in the dark. Messages sent out into space are consumed by the infinite reaches of the universe.

But that's not what God designed prayer to be. Our heavenly Father wants us to do more than just send up an emergency signal on those occasions when our life is falling apart. He wants a dialogue. He's not just the Sovereign sitting on His throne in some galaxy light years away. He's also the very present Companion. The One who promises to draw close to us when we pray.

The How-to of Successful Prayer

So if you want to really experience God in prayer, start by simply talking to God. Turn cries of desperation into friendly conversation. Realize that God is right beside you listening, wanting to teach you so that you can really grow in Him.

Now, there's one thing that keeps some of us from developing this sense of a friendly conversation, this sense of someone beside us listening. And that's simply that our mind wanders when we pray. It's quite natural for that to happen. We've got our eyes closed, perhaps we're leaning against our bed, and we're trying to carry on an interior monologue with God—and other thoughts keep interrupting. Our prayer keeps fading away into other things.

There's something very simple that you can do to keep your mind from wandering during prayer. It's something that I've done regularly, and it's really enhanced my own prayer life. Pray out loud. Secret prayer doesn't necessarily mean silent prayer. Jesus prayed out loud on more than one occasion. Now, don't worry that some demon's going to be listening to you. The devil flees at the sound of earnest prayer. God shuts us in with angels.

When we pray out loud, we become more conscious of what we're saying to God; we put more energy into what we're expressing. Try it. Just saying prayers out loud can go a long way toward keeping your mind on track. When the disciples discovered Jesus praying in a quiet, country place, they heard His petitions to His heavenly Father. They were so impressed with what they heard that when He stopped, they urged Him to "teach us to pray." Jesus then magnificently crafted "The Lord's Prayer." Repeatedly throughout His life, Jesus prayed aloud (see Luke 11:1; Matthew 26:39, 42, 44).

There's another thing we can do, too—use Scripture in prayer, use the Bible as subject matter for prayer. For example, read and meditate on a psalm, and then paraphrase some of its expressions as your own praise to God. Take a verse that strikes you, a verse that's very personal to you, even a key word in a verse, and concentrate on that as your appeal to God. Using Scripture in prayer gives us a sense of two-way conversation.

Dialogue with God need not be lengthy to be meaningful. It need not be flowery in language or elaborate in form. Trust Him to interpret what it is you are trying to say.

A woman I know uses the password "prayer" for her computer in the office. And each morning as she turns on the computer at the start of another hectic day, she is reminded to offer a simple one- or two-line prayer. Sometimes it's a line of praise, sometimes a supplication, sometimes a meditation. By associating the act of prayer with a common daily task, we can be reminded to pray to invite God to be with us in whatever that day brings.

Prayer and Praise

What is Paul's pattern for successful prayer? Is there some secret formula he reveals? Not at all. He simply says, pray! Pray on all occasions. Pray all kinds of prayers. Pray your sorrows, pray your joys, pray your challenges, pray your longings, pray your successes. Pray about everything. Communicate! Get a dialog going with the highest intelligence in the universe.

There is one quality that stands out, however, in New Testament prayer. Persistent prayer's most common companions are the twins: joy and thankfulness.

The apostle Paul's abundance of prayer, for example, flowed in a current of rejoicing. Listen to him: "I . . . do not cease to give thanks for you, making mention of you in my prayers" (Ephesians 1:15, 16, NKJV). Thankfulness—an ingredient of a vibrant prayer life. "We give thanks to the God and Father . . . praying always for you" (Colossians 1:3, NKJV).

Joy is another quality of prayer in Paul's ministry. "Always in every prayer of mine making request for you all with joy" (Philippians 1:4, NKJV).

The flood of prayer that brims over in the epistles is full-spirited, a joyful fountain ascending from the heart. Do you know why? Because that's the kind of prayer that's sustainable. Whining isn't. We tend to burn out when our petitions are aimed at the negative things we're trying to avoid. What God wants us to do most is focus on a positive goal. God is a solution-centered being.

A remarkable woman named Darlene Rose shows us what a difference that kind of prayer can make in practical life—even in the worst circumstances. Three long years of captivity had worn down the inmates of Kampili Prison, a notorious women's prison camp the Japanese had set up after their conquest of the Celebes Islands. World War II dragged on and on and on. The internees were threatened both by starvation and by bombing raids. Most had grown apathetic, and many were completely demoralized.

But one prisoner had a secret resource. Darlene Rose, a former missionary to New Guinea, had cultivated the habit of dialoguing with her heavenly Father. And she responded to the crisis by going on the offensive through prayer. One topic of Darlene's prayer life included Mr. Yamaji. He was the brutal camp commander who could beat prisoners unmercifully.

One day, standing before Mr. Yamaji in his office, Darlene had the opportunity to share a few words about the Almighty Creator who died even for him. To her amazement, she saw tears begin to trickle down his cheeks. He rushed into an adjoining room and closed the door. Darlene, again, prayed silently as she heard the commander weeping. After that, Mr. Yamaji began to show kindness to her and even tried to improve the camp conditions for everybody.

Darlene could very easily have fixed her attention on the unending disaster of imprisonment in her prayers. She could have prayed, "Please get us out of here; end this horrible war!" She could have sent up desperate signals into the dark. That would have been quite understandable under the circumstances.

But God would have seemed quite distant during those years in Kampili. Maybe He would come to the rescue someday, but not here today, nor tomorrow, nor next week. She would have found herself in that familiar plight: always crying out, never getting an answer. Instead, Darlene concentrated on what God could do right there in the camp. And what stands out in this woman's recollections of that time were acts of providence that lighted up the long night like a flare gun.

One night she couldn't keep from praying about an overwhelming craving for a banana she'd seen someone sneak in to another prisoner. "Lord, just one banana," she prayed, as she gave thanks for her rice porridge. And then, the next morning, a guard inexplicably walked into her cell and dropped a large cluster of bananas at her feet. Darlene slowly counted ninety-two of the precious fruit. God was real and present for Darlene Deibler Rose in a place where He could have seemed agonizingly distant. She found Him in the here and now because she looked there.

Darlene longed for the end of the war. Yet even as she longed for the deliverance she believed would soon come, Darlene was able to survive the present through faith and prayer and Bible study. Her spirits soared from the hardship of that prison camp to the joy of fellowship with God through prayer. Here was the stuff of survival. Here was a woman who could look up at the stars one night from a bomb-blackened shelter and rejoice that the Creator of the heavens had entered into a relationship with her. Here was a woman who could write these words, "Oh, the wonder of His love for me and His personal concern for me, as an individual, was overwhelming."

Have you found a God who can be this close? Have you tasted any of the heavenly Father's generous gestures? Or are you still sending desperate signals up into the vast darkness of space, just hoping against hope to make contact?

Why not begin a meaningful dialogue right now? God is so eager to "tell you great and unsearchable things you don't know." He's eager to be the still small voice next to your heart, instead of just the Sovereign somewhere in the universe.

But you have to make an investment, a serious investment in communication. Receiving signals from heaven isn't a matter of luck; you don't just happen to stumble across the right divine channel. You have to let God create a channel in your heart. You have to trust Him enough to believe that He *is* communicating with you right now and listen for and to His voice. You have to invest time in personal prayer, in discovering Him in His Word, time rejoicing in His presence. As you do, you will thrive in the problems of your life today and experience the inner spiritual strength to survive the overwhelming crisis headed straight for us tomorrow.

> Why are so many people turning to the psychics for guidance today? Can we really have confidence in the predictions of these self-proclaimed prophets of the future? Could this explosion of interest in the supernatural be a sign of the coming of Christ?

CHAPTER

SEVEN

Revelation Challenges the Psychics

On March 2, 1994, America got its most dramatic televised introduction to psychics and their prophecies. Never before, to my knowledge, has a major television network run a two-hour, prime-time special on this subject. And perhaps never before has so much been made out of such a small amount of evidence.

The program had a disclaimer that preceded the opening sequence, and it did imply that this would not be an objective evaluation of psychic prophecy. Nonetheless, the extent to which psychics were made to look like accurate predictors of the future was mind-boggling. Throughout the program, one extraordinary fact was ignored—the very poor track record of psychic prophecy as a whole.

In this chapter, I'd like to focus on the picture these people give us of the end of the world. Because here is where we come to the great collision between two contrasting views of the apocalypse or the end.

Psychics' Predictions

Now, here is the picture.

Some psychics say there is a cosmic time line running though Egypt's Great Pyramid. And the year 2000 is marked by a gaping pit in the floor of an underground chamber. This, they say, symbolizes a cataclysmic event at the end of this century.

The sixteenth century astrologer Nostradamus predicted that two-thirds of the world would be destroyed by a plague.

The twentieth-century psychic Edgar Cayce, who was known as "the sleeping prophet," predicted that the poles would shift, reversing the earth's magnetic fields, turning frigid lands to tropical ones, and vice versa. Coastlines would be covered by the sea. Many students of his writings believe that he expected this to happen before the year 2000.

Many psychics are predicting a cosmic disaster waiting for us—and the prime time television program suggested it may come around the year 2000.

Bible Prophecies

Now, let's look at another source of prophecy, one that has a much better track record than all the psychics put together. Bible prophecy is something we can test objectively. We can know that its predictions were written hundreds, sometimes thousands, of years before the predicted events. And some of the fulfillments of Bible prophecy have been spectacular—from the rise of the Messiah and specific details surrounding Jesus' death, to the succession of world empires, from Babylon to Medo-Persia to Greece to Rome.

So it makes sense to check out Bible prophecy. It's a source that claims to be written from God's all-seeing perspective.

The particular book of the Bible that focuses most on the end time is the apostle John's Revelation.

What does the Bible say about how the world will end? Well, at first glance there may not seem to be much of a collision between Revelation and the prophecies of the psychics. The apostle John also pictures cataclysms at the end of time. Revelation tells us of a great earthquake, of stars falling, the sun turning black, locusts that sting like scorpions, terrible plagues, and widespread devastation. So, yes, Revelation does warn of disasters at the end of the world. In fact, most psychic prophecies about the final cataclysm borrow images from this book.

But there's one big difference where the two types of prophecy collide. When psychics and occult seers look at the book of Revelation, they don't get the full picture. They don't latch onto the most important piece of the puzzle.

All the smoke and fire and disaster in Revelation form a backdrop that sets the stage for the real drama. The apostle John brushes jagged, dark strokes on the picture only to highlight the central scene, which reveals the central character.

Revelation is not about disaster; it's about Jesus Christ. It's about His coming back again. This is the event that makes sense out of all the symbols and figures and scenes in the book. Without Jesus Christ, Revelation has no meaning at all; all its prophecies are pointless.

Look in the very first chapter, and this is what you find: "Behold, He [Jesus] is coming with clouds, and every eye will see Him" (Revelation 1:7, NKJV).

What the Prophecies Point To

At the end of the world, what is everyone going to be looking at? Jesus Christ descending from heaven. That's the focus of attention.

And that's why the force of Scripture, the force of its final book, Revelation, is on a collision course with all the psychic and occult prophecies. They leave out the one thing that matters most—Jesus Christ. To talk about the earth crumbling and the sky falling, without talking about Jesus, is to paint a meaningless picture.

Now let's be honest—the New Age seers and psychics are not the only ones who have created a distorted picture of the end. Many Christians get lost among all the woes and plagues and beastly creatures. They get so caught up in trying to plot the right end-time sequence that they lose sight of what the picture is all about. They're fearful and afraid of the events that will soon come. So let me say it again—without Jesus Christ, Revelation has no meaning. All its prophecies are pointless.

Many people accept the fact that Jesus *should* be the central theme. But you may wonder if Jesus Christ really is at the center of all these apocalyptic scenes in Revelation. Sometimes they can appear rather gloomy and gruesome. Let me take you on a tour of some of the familiar highlights in the book of Revelation, and perhaps I can help you to see the book from a new perspective.

What Revelation Reveals

The very first words of Revelation are: "The Revelation of Jesus Christ." That's how John's book of prophecy got its name. It's a revelation *from* Jesus and *about* Jesus.

A few verses later, lest there be any doubt about who's at the center of this book, John presents Jesus Christ as "the faithful witness, the firstborn from the dead, and the ruler over the kings of the earth. To Him who loved us and washed us from our sins in His own blood . . . be glory and dominion forever and ever" (Revelation 1:5, 6, NKJV).

John goes on focusing on Christ as the Alpha and the Omega, the Beginning and the End. He pictures Christ as a glorious figure walking in the midst of lampstands, as the Master knocking on the door of our hearts, as the sacrificial Lamb of God. In chapter five, he describes heavenly beings who fall down before Him and proclaim "Worthy is the Lamb who was slain . . . Blessing and honor and glory and power . . . to the Lamb, forever and ever!" (Revelation 5:12, 13, NKJV).

Next in Revelation, we see Christ as the male Child born into the world who will rule all nations. (Revelation 12:1-5) In chapter 14, the Lamb of God reappears. He speaks with the voice of many waters, and thousands of the redeemed surround His throne.

In the next chapter, there is another scene of worship. Faithful believers stand on what looks like a sea of glass, and they sing the song of the Lamb, crying out: "Great and marvelous are Your works . . . Just and true are Your ways, O King of the saints!" (Revelation 15:3, NKJV).

Another series of apocalyptic scenes rushes by, and then Jesus appears yet again, riding out of the sky on a white horse, leading the armies of heaven. Revelation ends with a picture of heaven and the New Jerusalem, and the Lamb of God is at its center.

Are you beginning to get the picture? Perhaps you've always thought of the book of Revelation as a bunch of complicated symbols or the fearful vision of a holocaust. But that's not what the picture is about. Revelation puts the spotlight on Jesus—and it keeps it there.

In the End: Jesus

If you don't have Jesus at the end of the world, you don't have anything. Any series of prophecies or picture of the end times that doesn't focus on Christ is just plain wrong. It misses the whole point. That's why Revelation challenges the psychics. That's why the two kinds of prophecy collide. It is important to remember that the Bible does predict a catastrophe at the end of the world, which will include a time of trouble, the mark of the beast, and the seven last plagues. However, any focus on catastrophe that leaves out Jesus Christ misses the mark. These catastrophes serve to highlight the glory of Christ.

And what is Christ doing in the book of Revelation? He's coming again! Three times in the last chapter of the book of Revelation, Jesus declares, "I am coming quickly." He's returning to earth. He's leading the armies of heaven. He's a Conqueror, a Judge, a Saviour. Revelation is a wonderful promise, with Jesus' second coming as the main event. It's the one thing that gives meaning to the picture.

The artist and cartoonist Thomas Nast used to perform an interesting feat in public exhibitions. He took a canvas, six feet long by two feet wide, and placed it horizontally on an easel. Then he rapidly sketched a landscape with green meadows with cattle, fields of grain, a farmhouse, bright sky, and fleecy clouds. It was the usual cheery scene. When he stepped aside, the audience applauded.

Then Nast began to dab in a few darker colors, as if touching up the painting. Soon his strokes appeared reckless. He blotted out the bright sky, the fields and meadow. Dark slashes of paint obliterated the whole composition. It looked like something angry and abstract. Nast stepped back and declared, "It's finished."

The audience didn't know what to do—should they applaud or should they weep? Then Nast asked stage attendants to turn the canvas to a vertical position. And suddenly there stood a painting that depicted a beautiful waterfall, plunging over a cliff of dark rocks bordered by shrubs and trees. It was a stunning composition.

The picture of the end times can look quite scary. It can look quite chaotic—all those woes poured out, those trumpets of doom blasting, those plagues devastating the earth. It can appear like a dark series of clouds and slashes on the canvas.

But Jesus turns the picture right side up. He turns the whole planet right side up. Jesus, standing tall as the Alpha and the Omega, as the Bright and Morning Star, as the Leader of the armies of heaven coming to the rescue—that's what makes the picture of the end glorious and hopeful.

Final Judgment

But not for everyone. Not for everyone.

There's another reason why the prophecies of the book of Revelation and the prophecies of the psychics collide head on. There's another thing that psychics omit that is a very important part of the puzzle.

Listen to this final that which is given by an angel flying over the earth. In Revelation 14:7, he declares: "Fear God and give glory to Him, for the hour of His judgment has come" (NKJV).

The hour of His judgment has come. A final judgment—there's something that's not in the psychic vocabulary. The psychics and the seers seldom speak of the great cataclysm they see at the end of our century in moral terms. To them, it's not a great moment of truth for morally responsible individuals. It's just some disaster that will come.

In fact, the New Age mentality has more or less erased the whole idea of judgment. After all, we each have our own truth, they say. We're our own gods. Who's going to judge us?

Revelation challenges this kind of thinking in the most graphic terms. For John the apostle, the truth is that God is the Judge of the universe. Truth is not something we make up as we go along, but rather something that God reveals. It's God's idea of right and wrong, not ours, that matters. It's what matters now and in the end.

No, the second coming of Christ will not be a glorious event for everyone. For some it will be sheer terror.

In Revelation 6, John describes people who run and cry for the rocks and mountains to fall on them. This may seem like a gruesome and terrible event that causes you to say, "Well, here comes the fear again."

We must balance the pictures in Revelation that describe this fearful scene with the overtures of a loving God. Jesus, who comes to save, reaches out in love. He comes to judge sin and to eradicate it from the universe forever.

Revelation 6:15-17 says they "hid themselves in the caves and in the rocks of the mountains, and said to the mountains and rocks, 'Fall on us and hide us from the face of Him who sits on the throne and from the wrath of the Lamb! For the great day of His wrath has come, and who is able to stand?' " At the end of the world, some individuals would rather have rocks fall on them than meet Christ face to face. How tragic! They've turned their backs on Him in life, and they are afraid to face Him in death.

Revelation is not about an indifferent cataclysm. It's not about the blind forces of nature destroying earth. It's about human destiny. It's about where we're going to spend eternity. And everything depends on what we do about the central figure in the picture. Everything depends on what we do about Jesus.

Today, the followers of a woman named Elizabeth Clair Prophet are digging bomb shelters in order to prepare for the end. They think they're ready to survive Armageddon.

But that's not how our destiny will be decided. The apostle John has a different suggestion. He identifies the survivors of the end times in this way: "These are the ones who come out of the great tribulation, and washed their robes and made them white in the blood of the Lamb" (Revelation 7:14, NKJV).

How do we "come out of the great tribulation?" How do we survive Armageddon? By the blood of the Lamb. Our rescue doesn't depend on the strength of our bomb shelters—it depends on our relationship with the Lamb of God.

To wash our robes and make them white in the blood of the Lamb is a symbolic way of saying that we must accept the forgiveness that Jesus Christ offers through His sacrifice on the cross. It's a way of saying that the righteousness of the Lamb can cover us like a spotless white garment. It's a way of saying that the power of Jesus Christ is entered into our lives—that we have become victors over Satan by the power of Christ.

Today, Jesus reaches out to you. He appeals, "My child, come to Me today and open your heart to Me. I want to be your Lord and your Saviour and carry you through the end time. The apocalypse for you can be a glorious event rather than a terrifying one."

It's our response to the Living Lord, the Beginning and End, the King of kings, the Lamb of God, who will make all the difference in the end.

What happens when you die—do you go straight to heaven, hell, or nowhere? Is it just a matter of personal opinion? Is life after death a big question mark? Can the dead communicate with the living? Is it possible for demons to impersonate dead loved ones? Will Satan use this method to deceive in the last days? Discover the truth about life after death in these pages.

CHAPTER

EIGHT

The Truth About Near-Death Experiences

When Grace arrived at the hospital, she was shaking with fever and in terrible pain. Her insides seemed to be ripping apart, and she was slipping into septic shock. Just as she lost consciousness, she heard a voice yelling, "I can't get her blood pressure!"

And then, in the next moment, Grace felt like she was slipping out of her body and away from the pain. She seemed to be floating at the ceiling, watching doctors and nurses frantically trying to save her life.

Next, she turned toward a partially transparent cloud-like enclosure that formed a tunnel. Grace recalled the experience in these words:

I began to feel the most incredible warm, golden, loving

feeling . . . I was in this light . . . there was a presence in the light, a wisdom. . . . The wisdom loved me and at the same time it knew everything about me. Everything I had ever done and felt was there for me to see. I wanted to proceed into the light and stay there forever, but I was shown that I had to go back and take care of my two children.

With that thought, Grace felt she was back in her body, back in all the pain. She felt angry to be ripped away from the most wonderful peace in all the universe.

Grace's "Near-Death Experience," and many others, were reported in a recent *Life* Magazine article by Verlyn Klinkenborg ("At the Edge of Eternity," 19 March 1992, 65-73). NDE's (Near-Death Experiences) have become quite a hot topic lately. *Life After Life*, one of the first books on the subject, has sold a whopping seven million copies.

A few years ago, only a few individuals on the edge of science were interested in the topic. Now dozens of physicians, psychologists, biologists, and anthropologists are doing NDE research. There's actually a *Journal of Near-Death Studies* and an International Association for Near-Death Studies. Pollsters now estimate that some eight million Americans have had near-death experiences.

Where Do We Go?

What are we to make of all this? Just what does happen to people who seem to take incredible journeys at the moment of near death? Are these just hallucinations? Are they beginnings of an actual journey toward heaven and God? Or is there something occult, even demonic, involved in this shadowy other world of floating spirits?

Now, I'm certainly no expert on what happens to human beings physiologically at the moment of near death, but I believe that all of us can make a few common-sense judgments on the basis of the evidence. First of all, we have to remember one thing about all the people who relate NDE's: none of them really died. As physicians tell us, you're not dead when your heart stops or when you cease to breathe. You're dead when so many brain cells have died that there's just no chance of reviving you.

Secondly, many NDE's resemble hallucinations. The mind can play extraordinary tricks on us—especially at a time of great trauma. This is well documented in medical literature. Our brain can take us on vivid journeys to places that are real—and to places that are not real.

But here's the most important piece of evidence. The Bible does not teach that human beings have an immortal soul that leaves the body at the time of death. In fact, Scripture clearly states that we receive immortality only after the second coming of Jesus Christ.

The Bible's Teaching on Death

Paul states it plainly: "The Lord himself shall descend from heaven with a shout . . . and the dead in Christ shall rise first" (1 Thessalonians 4:16).

The Bible consistently teaches that death is a sleep with no conscious thought—a sleep that only Christ's coming disturbs. In fact, the Scripture refers to death as a sleep no less than fifty-three times. And although the King James Version of the Bible refers to the human soul some 1,600 times, it never once says the soul is immortal. Immortality is a quality God alone has (1 Timothy 6:16). We seek for immortality (Romans 2:6, 7). We will receive immortality only at the second coming of Christ (1 Corinthians 15:51, 52).

Jesus always referred to death as a temporary sleep until the resurrection. What happens at death? The Bible teaches that "the living know that they shall die, but the dead know not anything" (Ecclesiastes 9:5). At creation, God breathed the breath of life into human beings (Genesis 2:7), which enables us to live. When an individual dies, the breath (life-giving energy of God) returns to God (Ecclesiastes 12:7; Job 27:3). It is not something conscious. It is not something that thinks or feels. At death the thoughts perish (Psalm 146:4). Individuals who have died do not praise God (Psalm 115:17). Death is a momentary sleep until the glorious resurrection morning (1 Thessalonians 4:16, 17).

So there's one possibility that we can rule out altogether. And that's the idea that people at near death are actually being taken by God to heaven—that in some mysterious way He's drawing the disembodied soul up to its home in paradise.

The Enemy's Plan

Let's ask some tough questions. Who would develop a plan to disseminate ideas contrary to the biblical teaching on death—one that rewards everyone who dies with the joyous ecstasy of eternity, regardless of what they've done on earth? How could unrepentant child molesters, serial killers, porn kings, and mafia chiefs all feel acceptance in the presence of this eternal being of light?

Could this whole idea of NDE's be a ploy of the enemy to subtly suggest that it doesn't make much difference how you live? This is contrary to the Scriptures, which state: "It is appointed for men to die once, but after this the judgment" (Hebrews 9:27, NKJV).

Did you notice—"After this the judgment." First there's

death, and then there's judgment. Is it possible that powerful occult forces are at work in these NDE's? There is nothing mentioned about conversion, nothing mentioned about a Saviour, nothing about salvation, the cross, or redemption.

Near-death experiences portray a future that is contrary to the plain teaching of Scripture, which clearly teaches there is no salvation without Jesus Christ.

What kind of God would mistakenly start to bring Grace's soul to heaven and then, when hospital personnel managed to revive her, say, "Uh-oh, I made a mistake, I better put the soul back in the body again." God doesn't have trouble with His timing. He knows exactly when we're going to die.

The Bible rules out soul travel. But it gives us something much better. It shows us a very specific picture of life after death. Near-death experiences, as a rule, are like hazy dreams, but the Bible gives us the authentic account of what is to come. It's more than a window; it's a description of the scenery itself. And some of the landscape of heaven may surprise you. It's rather different from what some near-death experiences suggest.

The Near-Death Vision

In order to see the contrast between biblical hope and human imagination, let's follow a typical near-death journey and see where it leads. The first thing that many people report is a sensation of leaving the body, of floating above the scene. They become, in other words, a disembodied spirit.

Now, I don't know how you feel about existence as a disembodied spirit, but it has never appealed to me. How would you like to go through eternity as a ghost, wafting through the heavens, floating on the clouds?

For me, if you don't have a body, if you're just some kind of mind in space, then you're not really there. You've been cheated out of what God has planned.

Real Bodies

The Bible presents us with a vastly different picture. It tells us that after the resurrection, we are going to have very real bodies.

Let's take a look at a passage that deals with this subject in detail. First Corinthians 15, a great chapter on the resurrection. In verse 37, Paul likens death and resurrection to different kinds of seeds planted in the ground, which rise up as various kinds of grain, various kinds of "bodies."

He says that men have one kind of flesh, and fish and birds have another kind of flesh. He states that there are terrestrial bodies and celestial bodies. The implication is that the celestial body is more glorious than the one that we have here on earth, but it's very, very real.

Paul continues on with the words: "So will it be with the resurrection of the dead. The body that is sown is perishable, it is raised imperishable . . . it is sown in weakness, it is raised in power; it is sown a natural body, it is raised a spiritual body" (1 Corinthians 15:42-44, NIV).

Notice the Bible's emphasis on a real body. Commenting on Jesus' resurrection, the apostle Paul gives us this insight—our vile body will be changed like His glorious body (see Philippians 3:21). Christ's glorious body was certainly real. His disciples recognized Him. He walked and talked and ate with them.

The Bible doesn't picture for us an afterlife of disembodied spirits floating around. It shows us a world of real people with real bodies, stronger, more beautiful, more glorious than we have now. That's not just a dream; that's the reality.

Now let's return to the second part of a typical near-death journey. Many people report going through a long, dark or cloudy tunnel. There's rarely any definable scenery along the way; there's very little sense of place. It's a vague trip through space.

One woman who collapsed on the sidewalk one day and almost died reported this sensation: "I found myself surrounded by a dense, warm, foggy, gray material. In the fog I could see individual droplets of penetrating lightness and droplets of unfathomable darkness."

May I suggest that whatever this foggy tunnel may represent, the Bible offers us a much better picture of the afterlife; one that's sharply in focus. What do we see in the biblical concept of the afterlife?

Heaven Is an Actual Place

Listen to what John the Revelator reports: "Then I, John, saw the holy city, New Jerusalem, coming down out of heaven from God, prepared as a bride adorned for her husband" (Revelation 21:2, NKJV).

What did this disciple of Jesus Christ see on the other side of death? Much more than a tunnel. He saw an entire city coming down toward us, gleaming as brightly as a bride at her wedding. This city is so wonderful that, in trying to describe it, John simply exclaimed that its streets are pure transparent gold, its gates pearls, and the glory of God so bright that no night exists there.

The Bible gives us much more than a journey through

the fog. It offers us a place, a home. I really like the assurance that Jesus gave His disciples shortly before His crucifixion. "In My Father's house are many mansions . . . I go to prepare a place for you" (John 14:2, NKJV).

Jesus is preparing a *place* for us. Real people with real bodies, enjoying a real place, a real home in heaven. Are you beginning to see the difference between human dreams and the real thing?

Let's move to the final stage in most near-death experiences.

As people sense they're passing through a long cloudy tunnel, they see a light at the other end. The light comes closer, sometimes it envelops them quite dramatically.

A wounded soldier in Vietnam suddenly saw a massive bright light permeate the MASH unit room where the medics were working to revive him.

A Kansas woman reported: "Suddenly there was an explosion under me and reaching out to the farthest limits of my view was this light . . . the sun is not as bright . . . It filled up everything, and I was in the center of it."

Now these experiences can be quite meaningful for the individuals involved. It may even give them a sensation of God's love. But I'd like to suggest that Scripture offers something superior.

When we look at life after death in the Bible, we see much more than a bright light; we see a face—the glorious face of Jesus Christ. That's the great excitement, the sense of anticipation that fills the New Testament. That's the great hope that animated the early believers—a face-to-face encounter with the Living Christ.

No more stirring words have been penned than those of

John the Revelator when he describes those who come before the throne of God in heaven: "They shall see his face" (Revelation 22:4). They shall see His face. That's what awaits those who have made friends with Christ the Saviour in this life.

Paul puts it eloquently in his classic chapter on Christian love: "Now we see in a mirror, dimly, but then face to face" (1 Corinthians 13:12, NKJV). That's a great hope to have in this life. That's something to look forward to. It's more than looking through a foggy window; it's more than a dream. It's the real thing—a face-to-face encounter with Jesus Christ.

Near-death experiences may offer us tantalizing suggestions about the next life. But let's remember, the Bible doesn't just hint at some journey. It shows us the scenery. It doesn't just suggest a semideath after death—it proclaims life in all its abundance after death. Not just a disembodied spirit, but a genuine body to move in. Not just a cloudy tunnel, but a resplendent city to live in. Not just a bright light, but a loving Saviour to love and enjoy forever.

A Real Hope

Does the New Testament hope make a difference? I believe it makes all the difference in the world.

That came through to me very clearly during my recent trip to Russia for meetings in Moscow's Olympic Stadium. There I met a woman whom I'll call Tanya, who told me about her family. Years before, her parents had emigrated to China and become wealthy in the tea business. After some time, they decided to return to Russia, and they established their tea business in Kazakhstan.

Just as it was beginning to flourish, Stalin began his purges of the elite and wealthy. When Tanya was 17, her father was taken out of the house by the secret police and shot through the head. Later, during the Second World War, her brother, sister, and husband were killed. Within a matter of two years, she had lost everyone closest to her.

Tanya struggled with depression. She attended an English school and eventually became fluent in the English language. Toward the end of the Second World War, the Russians needed translators in the military, so she became a translator for one of the American generals.

Tanya had come from an Orthodox Jewish background, but had little interest in religion because of the horrors of war. Through the years, she did rather well for herself, advancing in educational and diplomatic circles. Yet she always sensed that something was missing in her life. She could never come to terms with all the suffering her family had experienced, and she couldn't accept the terrible finality of their cruel deaths.

One day, someone on the street handed Tanya a brochure advertising a Christian evangelistic effort. She attended the meetings and there accepted Christ as her Saviour. She found a new peace and meaning in her life.

Tanya was much happier as a believer, but there was still something she couldn't quite grasp. Why would a loving God permit so much suffering? What really happens when you die? Not all the pieces seemed to fit together in the puzzle.

One day as she passed the Olympic Stadium in Moscow, she saw a large sign proclaiming "The Bible Way to New Life" and picked up a brochure. After reading it, she decided to check out the meetings.

Tanya was there night after night, including the night I spoke on the subject of Jesus' soon return. After the meeting, she came up to me and said, "Pastor, I was deeply moved tonight." And she began showing me old photographs of her family and telling me about their tragic deaths.

Her face was beaming as she exclaimed, "Now I can look forward to seeing them again." She wasn't brokenhearted any longer.

Tanya wasn't just looking forward to an out-of-body experience. She wasn't looking forward to a trip through a cloudy tunnel or a glimpse of a brilliant, vague form of light. She was looking forward to face-to-face reunions in a very real place with very real people.

She was also looking forward to the specific day when Jesus Christ will break through the clouds, the time that Jesus Christ will change history once again and take His followers back with Him to heaven, the place that He's prepared for them.

Tanya was looking forward to that ultimate reunion. And she was among the 700 individuals who committed their lives to Christ in baptism one unforgettable day in Moscow.

Don't you want to have that kind of assurance in your life? Don't you want to be able to look forward to a face-to-face reunion with family, loved ones, friends, and Jesus Christ? Don't you want to tap into that full supply of love the Saviour has for you?

God has more for you than a vague journey through a mystical tunnel that leads to a being of light in a misty place.

He has heaven, eternity, a real city, a real world, a real body, a real Saviour. He longs for you to be there with Him through all eternity.

Have you ever had a desire to belong? Have you felt an emptiness inside longing for home? Each of us yearns to know that there is somewhere we can belong and someone we can belong to. In this chapter you'll learn the amazing truth that God has given us a place today to prepare for eternity tomorrow.

CHAPTER
NINE

Somewhere I Can Belong

The first time I saw her, something happened inside me. She moved down the street with a peculiar shuffle, her eyes glued to the sidewalk. It was obvious from her gray hair and wrinkles that she was old. But there was something more. She was weathered, worn, and dirty. The odor emanating from her body was foul. Her unwashed clothes and unkempt hair were a tragic sight. She pushed a battered shopping cart filled with plastic bags and cardboard.

I see her regularly in the elite community of Thousand Oaks, California—the homeless woman. Each time I see her, I feel a tinge of pain. My teenage son tells me she wanders aimlessly from Ventura to Newbury Park, on to Thousand Oaks and to Westlake and back again. She has no place to live, no place to belong.

A Need Inside

I do not know her particular situation. Perhaps alcoholism consumed all her money. Perhaps she is mentally ill. Perhaps she was severely abused by a parent or a husband. Whatever the cause of her homelessness, her plight haunts me. Here's why. Inside all of us is the need to belong somewhere. And homeless people don't have a place. They don't belong somewhere. You know that instinctively. That's why it's hard to turn our eyes away. Sometimes, even if we live in a beautiful four-bedroom dream house, we still find ourselves looking for that place to feel secure, a place to feel contented.

Think of all the different clubs and associations there are in America. Dog-breeders' clubs, country clubs, tennis clubs, karate studios. We've got everything from coin collectors' clubs to support groups for people who claim to have been kidnapped by aliens. Why? Because people are looking for a place to fit in. A place to belong.

Consider the many ethnic conflicts around the world. Many are caused by the desire for a place to belong. Different people claim to have their roots in a particular turf. That is their identity. Many are willing to kill and die in order to possess it. The city of Jerusalem is bound up in the identity of the Arabs, the Jews, and the Christians. Conflicts explode over a piece of geography because it represents a place of belonging. A place we can belong is an endless human quest.

Personally, I believe that God has created just such a place for us. It's not a geographical location accessible only to some. It's what one author called "a palace in time" reachable by everyone. It's a day that God set aside for us at the very beginning of time, at Creation. A certain day where we can discover our true identity. Something unique happened on the seventh day of Creation. During the first six days, God clothed this planet with fruit-bearing trees and lush vegetation. He made a home for the first two human beings. On the seventh day, He gave them something else. Genesis 2:3 (NKJV) states, "Then God blessed the seventh day and sanctified it." When God wrote the Ten Commandments with His own finger on tables of stone, He stated in the fourth commandment, "Remember the sabbath day, to keep it holy" (Exodus 20:8). Remember your roots. Remember where you belong. Remember your Creator. Remember your identity.

The Sabbath—a Place of Belonging

The Sabbath reveals that we have been created in the image of God. The Sabbath takes us back to a perfect world, revealing that we did not evolve. We're not merely a chemical combination of genes and chromosomes. We are unique, special, created in the image of God. The Sabbath shows us that we belong. It shows us that the Creator of the whole universe made us and fashioned us. The Sabbath reveals to us that we're special, that we're unique, that there's nobody else like us in the universe. We are more than accidental happenstance. We were specially formed by a loving God.

A number of years ago, one of my sisters, who will remain nameless, had a summer job editing high-school textbooks. This necessitated that she be away from her husband for a few weeks. Much of her day was spent photocopying material to be proofread. As she copied hundreds of pages, she became bored. Suddenly a bright idea struck her. Why not photo-copy her face and send it as a joke back to her husband. She put her face on the copy machine, then pushed the start button. The alarm went off. The paper jammed, the machine stopped. A service technician had to be called in. I've teased her about trying to photocopy herself ever since. It is true, though, you cannot produce a person on a photocopy machine. We are just not copyable.

Every human being is special and unique. If God loses me, I cannot be replaced. God cares for me. He is interested in me, and He loves me, and I am the only one of me he has. My love and praise ascend to Him through the uniqueness of my personality, marked with my specialness. No one can love, worship, and praise Him exactly like me.

The Sabbath calls us back to our roots. It calls us back to the fact that we're children of God. It's a link to our family of origin. The Sabbath has been observed continuously week after week since time began. It's an unbroken connection through time back to our Creator. The Sabbath tells us that we're not just a product of time plus chance. We're members of a family created by God. And that's important to know. In this day of rest, a sacred day that stretches back to the beginning of history, we take the time to get to know who we really are in the Father's eyes.

When Jesus was on earth, He spent time with His heavenly Father in praise and worship on the Sabbath. He was always conscious of who He was in God's eyes. Luke states "As his custom was, he went into the synagogue on the sabbath day, and stood up for to read" (Luke 4:16). The Sabbath is a perpetual reminder for us, as it was for Jesus, of who we really are. It reminds us of our origin. It keeps us focused on the glorious truth that we are children of God.

Rest in Christ

There is another sense in which the Sabbath reveals that we have someplace to belong. It shows us that we can rest in Christ. This is what the writer of Hebrews is referring to when he says "There remains therefore a rest for the people of God. For he who has entered His rest has himself also ceased from his works as God did from His" (Hebrews 4:9, 10, NKJV). Entering into Sabbath rest means that we cease from trying to create salvation on the basis of our own efforts. God has done the work for us in Christ. When Jesus voluntarily poured out His life on the cross, He died for us. He gave His perfect life as a substitute for our sinful life.

In a sense, this Carpenter from Nazareth built a special dwelling for us out of His righteousness. We can find refuge there. We can be safe there. His work is complete, it's finished. We can rest confidently in the forgiveness that Christ offers. We can know that in Christ we're accepted by the heavenly Father. The seventh-day Sabbath is not a legalistic requirement symbolizing a system of works. When we rest on the Sabbath, we are resting in Christ's love. We are resting in His care. We are resting in His righteousness.

Sabbath rest is a symbol of a faith experience in Jesus. It is a graphic illustration of our trust in Him. All week we work, but on the seventh day we rest. We turn from our works to a total rest in Christ. In Jesus, we have someplace to belong. We need not stressfully work out our own salvation. Our lives need not be filled with guilt and fear and anxiety. The Sabbath reveals the restful attitude. Salvation comes only through Jesus. We do not deserve it. We cannot earn it. We rest and receive it by faith. When Jesus breathed His last and cried, "It is finished," He closed His eyes and died. The work of redemption was complete. He rested on the Sabbath, symbolizing a completed or finished work. At the end of Creation week, God rested, symbolizing a finished work. Each Sabbath as we rest on the last day of the week, we, too, declare, "God, I am resting in the completed work of Christ on the cross. 'Nothing in my hand I bring, Simply to Thy cross I cling.' "

The Eden Life

There is still more that rounds out the picture. The prophet Ezekiel declares, "Moreover also I gave them my sabbaths, to be a sign between me and them, that they might know that I am the Lord that sanctify them" (Ezekiel 20:12). Here's another reason why God gave us the Sabbath. It shows that the Lord is the One who sanctifies us. How is that? Well, that's what God did to the seventh day. It was an ordinary slice of time just like any other at the end of Creation week, but God set this particular day apart. He sanctified it. And through the Sabbath, God tells us "that's what I want to do for you, too. I want to set you apart as my special child. I want to pour Myself into you. I want to sanctify you. I want to share my holiness with you."

God placed a special blessing in the Sabbath. As you and I keep the Sabbath, we receive God's blessing and experience His power in a way that is different than if we worship on any other day. All days are not the same. God blessed the seventh day. He sanctified it and rested on it, and hallowed it. In addition, God commanded us to keep the seventh day (Genesis 2:2, 3). When we enter into Sabbath rest as Christ commands, His Spirit blesses our lives as He promised.

The Sabbath reminds us of where we develop character— in relationship with our heavenly Father and with Jesus Christ. The Sabbath is a continual living promise of God's ability to help us grow through all the ups and downs, tragedies and triumphs, of our lives. We need that distinctive time with the heavenly Father. We need Sabbath quality time with the God who sanctifies us, the God who helps us keep growing.

The Earth Made New

This leads us to the final reason that God created this palace in time—one last piece in the puzzle that shows us what the Sabbath really means for us. "Hallow my sabbaths; and they shall be a sign between me and you, that ye may know that I am the Lord your God" (Ezekiel 20:20). The Sabbath is a sign of our relationship with the Lord. In other passages we learn that the Sabbath is a sign of a covenant between God and His people, their commitment to each other based on promises (see Ezekiel 20:12, 20; Exodus 31:17; Hebrews 4:9, 10). And above all, the covenant is eternal. In Exodus 31, God's people are urged to keep the Sabbath throughout their generations as a perpetual covenant. It's described as a sign between God and His children forever.

The Sabbath has continued in the weekly cycle from the dawn of Creation until now. The Sabbath began in the Garden of Eden, and the Sabbath will be celebrated when this earth is renewed after Christ's second coming. The prophet Isaiah talks about the time when God will make the "new heavens and the new earth." He says: " 'It shall come to pass that from one New Moon to another, and from one Sabbath to another, all flesh shall come to worship before Me,' says the Lord" (Isaiah 66:23, NKJV). The Sabbath beautifully represents a forever relationship with God. It stretches from the Garden of Eden at Creation to the garden that God will make of this planet at the end of time. It stretches from paradise lost to paradise restored.

We need that kind of forever in our lives. We need a place that reassures us that we are in an eternal relationship with the heavenly Father. We need a palace in time where that assurance can sink in deep, a place that says our heavenly Father will always be there for us. In the Sabbath, we can find a sense of contented rest. We can get in touch with our roots as His children there. We can grow and mature there. Yes, we need that kind of forever place that ties the whole of our lives to an eternal relationship with God.

He stated in the fourth commandment, "Remember the sabbath day, to keep it holy" (Exodus 20:8). The Sabbath command speaks to us gently, "Remember your roots. Remember where you belong. Remember your eternal destiny." Each week Jesus took a refreshing, reflective pause on the Sabbath. Our Saviour knew that the Sabbath refocuses our thinking on things eternal. It points us to the Almighty. It lifts our eyes from things below to things above. It points to a better land where all things are made new.

Revelation's final message for humanity is a clarion call to worship our Creator. The apostle John declares, "I saw another angel fly in the midst of heaven, having the everlasting gospel to preach unto them that dwell on the earth, and to every nation, and kindred, and tongue, and people, saying with a loud voice, Fear God, and give glory to him; for the hour of his judgment is come: and worship him that made heaven, and earth, and the sea, and the fountains of waters" (Revelation 14:6, 7). Heaven's final appeal just before the coming of Jesus is to worship our Lord as our life-giving Creator. The fact that He created us is the basis of all our worship (Revelation 4:11). The Sabbath is the golden chain that unites us to Him as our Creator, Redeemer, and coming King.

If your spiritual life is weak, perhaps it is because you have lost sight of the meaning of the Sabbath. Jesus' example calls us to intimate fellowship with the Father each Sabbath. If fellowship with His Father on Sabbath was a foretaste of eternity for Jesus, certainly it can be the same for us.

> What is the mysterious mark of the beast? How can we best prepare for the overwhelming events soon to burst upon our world? Know for yourself what is really going on and what is going to happen. This chapter draws aside the curtain across the future and enables you to view things through eyes of prophecy.

CHAPTER

TEN

Forever Marked

Steve Dickerson tells the story of Bill, who grew up on a farm. There was never any question about Bill's future. He'd be a farmer like his dad. He went to college and studied agriculture, which gave him the scientific know-how, but he worried about where he would get the money to buy a farm.

One day his father said, "Bill, I'm getting old. I'm almost ready to retire. I'd like to give the farm to you."

Bill was speechless. His problem was solved!

But the older man went on. "There's just one stipulation. I want you to run the farm strictly according to my directions for the first year. After that, it's yours."

That was fair enough. Dad was a good farmer. He knew what he was doing. And just think—after a year, the farm would be his!

The two men spent the next few days going from field

to field. Bill carried a notebook and wrote down just what his father wanted him to plant in each field. Then his father and mother left for a vacation.

Bill was curious. It would be interesting to see how his father's directions checked out with what he'd learned in college. He got out his soil-testing kit and started around the farm again. As he went from field to field, he was impressed with his father's wisdom. In each field, his dad had scooped up a handful of soil and examined it carefully before deciding what to plant, and he had been right every time. He had chosen the very crop that, according to what Bill had learned in college, would grow the best in that particular soil.

Every time, that is, until Bill came to the last field. His father had said to plant corn, but he must have made a mistake. The soil was sandy and poor. Plant corn? The shallow roots would be torn right out of the soil by the slightest wind. Even if the stalks weren't blown over, the corn would be sickly. Dad must have made a great mistake.

Bill's analysis showed that the soil would be much better for peanuts. *Dad would want every crop to be a success. He'd be pleased to see that all the money spent on his son's education had paid off,* Bill thought, so he planted peanuts.

At harvest time, Dad came back and said the farm had never looked so good. Bill took him around and showed him the wheat and the potatoes and the alfalfa.

"But where's the corn?" Dad wanted to know. "I thought I told you to plant corn."

Bill said, "Well, yes, Dad. That was in this field over here. I went back and tested the soil in all the fields. You were exactly right in all, except this one. So I thought you must have made a mistake. I was sure you would rather see a good crop of peanuts than a sickly crop of corn."

Dad shook his head sadly. "Bill," he said, "you haven't followed my directions in any of these fields. You've followed your own judgment in every case. It just happened that you agreed with me in all points except one. But as soon as there was any question, you did what you thought best in spite of what I had said. I'm sorry, Bill, but you'll have to look elsewhere for a farm of your own."

The father's reaction might seem harsh to us, but the story is a good illustration of how important it is for us to follow God's instructions—even when we don't fully understand why He has given them.

God's Instructions

God has written down on slabs of stone some specific directions for us. And on condition that we follow them, He promises not a farm, but a future beyond our wildest dreams, and never-ending life. We call those directions the Ten Commandments.

Unfortunately, millions today have brought out their own personal analyzing kits. They think it would be interesting to see how God's directions compare with what they've been taught at the university or with their own philosophy of life or sense of right and wrong. And what happens?

Millions today are improvising their own off-the-cuff morality to meet their moods. They've decided that God's directions are outdated and certainly not relevant for this enlightened generation. And even if they agree with God part of the time, they are sure that in some instances He has made a mistake. And so they're planting peanuts and thinking how pleased God will be when He sees the crop!

Unfortunately today, many people believe that God sometimes throws His Ten Commandments into reverse. They think it's all right to steal if you have an emergency. Or lie if it'll help keep you out of jail. Or commit adultery if, as philosopher Joseph Fletcher has suggested, having a child is the only way to get out of a concentration camp.

Too many people today follow God's directions when they agree with them and ignore the dictates when they don't seem to make sense.

If we obey only when we agree, have we obeyed at all? You remember the penetrating, thought-provoking words of Jesus in Matthew: "Not everyone who says to Me, 'Lord, Lord,' shall enter the kingdom of heaven, but he who does the will of My Father in heaven" (Matthew 7:21, NKJV).

God's Problem

That's what it means to serve God—doing the will of the Father in heaven. God has the same problem today that He had with our first parents. He wanted to give them never-ending life. But He dared not give them immortality without first testing their loyalty. He had to be sure they could be trusted with a life that never ends!

How could He do this? What sort of test could He devise that would give Him assurance of their loyalty? Promises were not enough. Promises are easy.

God could have put an active volcano, a crater of fire, on the edge of the Garden. He could have told Adam and Eve that to jump into it would mean death. And they would have stayed away from it, for sure. No, God must devise a test that, to human reasoning, seemed not to make sense. Obedience must stem from allegiance alone.

Let me illustrate. The story is told of a railroad worker who lived near the tracks. He looked up from his work one day to see his four-year-old son playing on the tracks while a train was thundering toward him!

There was no time to reach the boy and snatch him away. The father called, but Robert didn't hear. He called a second time, but Robert still didn't hear. He called at the top of his voice, for there was time for nothing else, "Robert, lie down and don't move!"

Robert obeyed instantly, without even turning to look his father's way. The train, barreling down the tracks, rushed over the motionless boy. After the caboose passed, the father gathered up the little boy, his little heart was pounding, but he was safe!

There was nothing in Robert's few short years to qualify him to understand his father's command. But he didn't delay. His father had spoken. And that was enough for him!

Just so, in Adam and Eve's experience there was nothing to qualify them to understand God's strange command. Why should the fruit of one tree, just as beautiful as the others, have death within it? They didn't understand that the seemingly unimportant act of eating the fruit clearly revealed the weakness of their loyalty.

God has the same problem today that He had in the Garden of Eden. Millions have professed their loyalty, but not all can be trusted with never-ending life. How else can their loyalty be tested except with a command that makes no sense to the human mind?

The Beast and His Mark

The thirteenth chapter of Revelation contains some very frightening predictions. There's a *beast* representing a nation, or a power. In this case, it's evidently a coalition of religious and political power.

There's a second beast, a nation that starts out with lamb-like characteristics but later speaks as a dragon. And this second beast is evidently a democracy, because it persuades the people to create an image of the first beast. This image, a coalition of religious and political power, pronounces a death sentence upon all who refuse to worship the first beast. And those who refuse to receive the mark of this beast are not permitted to buy or sell. Frightening, will you agree?

But in the fourteenth chapter of Revelation, in verses 6 through 12, we find God's last call to men. And in the message of the third angel, verses 9 to 11, we find the most fearful warning in all the Scriptures. It's a warning against worshiping the beast and his image or receiving his mark!

Now, this is not something to play games with. This business in the book of Revelation is extremely serious. It appears to be a matter of death-if-you-do and death-if-you-don't. No middle ground!

I'm aware of the widespread notion that the book of Revelation cannot be understood. But I ask you, would God include so fearful a warning in His last call to men if He knew that the identity of the beast and the nature of his mark could not be understood? Hardly!

God's Mark

But before we explore some clues as to what that mark might be, what about God? Does God have a mark too? John records these words in the book of Revelation: "After these things I saw four angels standing at the four corners of the earth, holding the four winds of the earth, that the wind should not blow on the earth . . . Then I saw another angel ascending from the east, having the seal of the living God. And he cried with a loud voice to the four angels . . . "Do not harm the earth . . . till we have sealed the servants of our God on their foreheads"

(Revelation 7:1-3, NKJV).

God, then, has a seal. He, too, has a mark. It seems evident that every man, woman, and youth will be asked to choose between the mark of God and the mark of the fallen angel, and by that choice declare loyalty to one or the other.

What will God's mark be? What test will God administer to His professed people that will reveal, once for all, who is safe to take into His kingdom and who is not, who can be trusted with never-ending life and who cannot? Certainly, it'll be something that has no foundation in human reason, a command that His true people will obey simply because God has spoken. That's the kind of test to look for.

True Loyalty

Has God given us such a command? If He has, there would be no more logical place to look for it than in Exodus 20, the Ten Commandments—God's moral code for all people and for all time.

The first three commands seem reasonable enough. If God is the true God, certainly we should not bow down to any other gods. God should certainly have our respect.

The last six commandments are so reasonable that for thousands of years they have frequently been incorporated into the laws of nations, including nations that don't worship the true God. Thou shalt not kill. Thou shalt not steal.

But one commandment, the fourth, is different. It doesn't fit into man's reasoning. There seems to be no moral principle involved. It seems quite arbitrary. The command would not be so troublesome if it simply asked for one day in seven as a day of rest. Most anyone would go along with the idea of a day off every seven days. Labor unions like it. Atheists like it. It certainly would not indicate any particular loyalty to God to take one day in seven for rest.

But the commandment specifies the seventh day. It is this specificness that makes it a problem and often makes it inconvenient. Certainly the days are all alike—twenty-four hours long. What difference does it make which day we devote to rest and worship? It doesn't seem logical that God should specify a particular day. But He has. And there will always be those who love Him enough to obey Him without asking why!

Could this be the test that we're looking for—a command that doesn't make sense to the human mind? It certainly fits. God, seemingly without reason, placed one tree in the center of Eden and declared it off-limits to our first parents. It was His test of their loyalty.

Could it be that God has placed in the center of His law a command that doesn't easily answer to human reason—and that in these final days He'll use that test as a measure of the loyalty of everyone who professes to follow Him?

Yes, the Sabbath commandment is unique among the ten. There is no controversy about the other nine. Most good citizens, Christian or not, will go along with them because they agree with them.

But does any person, regardless of how often he goes to church or how much he puts in the offering plate or how spotless his moral character, really obey God if he only obeys when he understands why? If a woman must comprehend the reason, agree with God, and make sense of the command before she obeys, does she really obey at all? No, like the farmer's son, she is really following her own judgment all the way!

God's Choice

Now I know that the identity of the day of rest may seem like a trivial matter. Surely, you say, there must be more important issues. But we cannot always choose our challenges. The fireman cannot choose the location of the fires he fights. The soldier cannot choose where he'll go to war. The lesson of many wars was this—that battles will not always be fought where they seem most likely.

The book of Revelation tells us that Satan is angry with the people who persist in keeping God's commands. That's what Revelation 12:17 says. Then I ask you, will Satan focus his attack on the commandments that people find reasonable and about which there is no controversy? Or will he zero in on the one commandment that doesn't answer to human reason, the one that rests on God's authority alone?

Do you begin to see what the mark of God might be—and what the mark of the beast might be?

If God uses the Sabbath commandment as a test of loyalty, and if a faithful observance of that command marks a man as one who can be trusted to go God's way forever, then what might be the mark of the opposite camp? I suggest to you that it might be a substitute Sabbath brought into the Christian church during the Middle Ages when the Scriptures were not available to people, a day of worship resting not on divine authority, but on human sanction. What could be more logical?

You see, the controversy isn't really over a day at all. It's over authority. Whose sovereignty will you accept—God's, or man's?

It matters not how trivial the command may appear. If God should say to you, "Go stand in the corner," and Satan should say, "Don't stand in the corner," it would probably seem downright ridiculous. But it would make a mighty big difference which command you obey, for it would mark you as a loyal follower of one or the other!

No one has the mark of the beast today. God will not permit any person to receive that mark until the issues are out in the open and each one clearly understands what is at stake.

Our Choice

Only when we recognize the critical nature of the step we are taking, if we deliberately choose to obey a human command in the place of a command of God, then our action will have marked our loyalty. The mark will be in the forehead if we believe the propaganda of Satan, or in the hand if we know it's false but go along with it anyway. The mark will be invisible to human beings, but angels of God will see it and know where our loyalty is!

And what of the mark of God? Even now, our attitude toward God and toward His commandments may decide our destiny. But at this moment, it has not become the final test of loyalty that it will be in the days ahead.

There are still too many people outwardly loyal to the commands of God, whose commitment is only for fair weather. When the predictions of Revelation 13 become a reality, when no man can buy or sell, when imprisonment and death are enforced, when it's no longer convenient to obey God, the superficial hangers-on will be shaken out.

And those who keep the faith even when their lives are threatened will be giving God evidence that they can be trusted with never-ending life. The mark of God will be in their forehead, in their mind. His mark is never received in the hand, for God only accepts the worship that comes from the heart and mind. Satan, on the contrary, doesn't care how he gets his worship. If he can't get it by choice, he'll try to get it through force.

The mark of God. And the mark of Satan. On the one hand, a command that is based solely upon the authority of God. On the other hand, a command that's based solely on the authority of men. This is the choice that's racing toward us!

Have we been weaving a fabric of guesswork here? Has there really been an attempt to change God's law? Is the challenge of God's authority about to surface openly? Yes, the prophet Daniel predicted it. Paul said it would come. Revelation spotlights it. And the power represented by the beast of Revelation 13 comes along and says in substance, "Yes, we did it. We're proud of it. We consider the act a mark of our authority."

One thing is certain. We're moving rapidly toward the day of final choices. The issue is God's law or man's tradition. It's more than a matter of days—it's a matter of faithfulness, obedience, and loyalty.

We are preparing for that final day by the little decisions, the seemingly insignificant choices we make along the way. If we habitually choose the easy way, the popular way, the way of the crowd, we shall find it only natural, in the crisis, to go along with the crowd.

We shall have some surprises when we see who is strong and who is weak. Some that we thought were so strong will prove miserably weak. And some that we thought were weak will display an incredible courage and be forever marked as friends of God!

How will it be with you? Deep within your own mind, have you settled it—that loyalty to God is what really matters? Deep within your own heart, have you made that decision to maintain your faithfulness to Christ no matter what anybody else does?

Where is America headed? Is the ink on the parchment of liberty fading? Will the American experiment in justice for all fail? Will our liberties be severely restricted in the near future? Is it possible that some in our country will experience imprisonment, torture, and death for their conscientious convictions? This shocking chapter unveils the truth through the eyes of prophecy.

CHAPTER

ELEVEN

When Liberty Fades

It was Tuesday morning, July 2, in Philadelphia. It had been raining hard since six o'clock. By nine o'clock, almost fifty delegates had arrived at the State House on Walnut Street, where the Second Continental Congress was in session. The room was steamy, but keeping the windows closed against the rain also kept out the horseflies from the nearby stable. For almost fifteen months, the colonists had been fighting the British without any formal declaration of war or even a formal declaration of independence.

But the people were becoming impatient, and the feeling for independence was running high. Yet it was not an easy thing to decide to cut much of the continent with its 2.5 million inhabitants free from the British Empire. It was felt that in such a weighty decision, the vote must be virtually unanimous. But the day before, after stirring debate, the vote had been indecisive. So the radicals had been work-ing feverishly to override the opposition. It seemed now that only Delaware was stalemated, with one delegate for, one against, and one back home on business. The secretary, Charles Thompson, began reading the resolution, ready for another vote. And then, over the wet cobblestones, came the sound of hoofbeats. Farmer Caesar Rodney, Delaware's third delegate, had heard that his delegation was deadlocked, and he had ridden all night to cast the deciding vote. Soak-ing wet, his face splattered with mud, he entered the hall and said simply, "The thunder and rain delayed me."

So it was that the Second Continental Congress voted unanimously for independence. All that was necessary now was to justify its stand before the world. Back in June, a tall red-haired Virginian, Thomas Jefferson, had been asked to prepare a draft of the declaration. The delegates would come together on July 4 to sign it.

Among the many legends of that day is one that tells of the old bell ringer. He had been told to be on hand to start ringing as soon as the word was out. Pessimistic, he waited with one hand on the rope in the old belfry and muttered, "They'll never sign it. They'll never sign it."

But sign it they did. The story has it that a little boy was stationed outside the great colonial door. Watching through the huge keyhole, he saw a movement of chairs and heard the shuffle of excited feet. Running to the bell tower he shouted, "Ring, Grandpa, ring for liberty." The Declara-tion of Independence raised the sights and objectives of a new nation. It set a new standard for a free society. It was a lofty ideal and a long-range goal.

The Declaration was really a promise, a promise of lib-erty, a promise of freedom, a promise of a republican/democratic form of government. Years later, we inscribed these words of Emma Lazarus on the Statue of Liberty—"Give me your tired, your poor, your huddled masses yearning to breathe free."

America is synonymous with political and religious freedom. But could this freedom be lost even in a land dedicated to its protection? Could it be carelessly sacrificed upon a modern altar of conformity? Are subtle forces, all but unnoticed, forging handcuffs for the consciences of mankind?

Those early framers of the Declaration of Independence were guided not by their own thoughts, but by God. When the Pilgrims courageously left Europe on the Mayflower and crossed the Atlantic to the unknown world of America, they wanted to escape the totalitarian religious oppression of the past. They longed to be free from persecution, free from the fires of tyranny. They wanted to found a country where they would be free to worship God and practice the religion they believed in. When the boat pulled into the harbor off Plymouth, Massachusetts, and the first band of Pilgrims set foot on this continent, they knelt to thank God for their safe journey.

Freedom's Flag Unfurled

The flag of the United States stands tall. The framers of our Constitution made clear statements about the separation of church and state. They had seen the abuses of the system in Europe and wanted to prevent such things from happening in the nation they were forming. George Washington said in 1789, "Every man conducting himself as a good citizen and being accountable to God alone for his religious opinion, is to be protected in worshiping the Deity according to the dictates of his own conscience."

Ben Franklin put it this way: "When religion is good I can see that it will support itself. And when it cannot support itself, and God does not take care to support it, so that its professors are obliged to call for the help of the civil power, it is a sign, I apprehend, of its being a bad one." Ben Franklin's point is well taken. Any religion that can't rely upon God and must appeal to the government for support must not be very good.

Ulysses S. Grant, Civil War general and president in the 1800s said, "Leave the matter of religious teaching to the family altar, the church, and private schools supported entirely by private contributions. Keep the church and state forever separate." The United States was built on the principle of individuals worshiping in harmony with the dictates of their own consciences and the principle of tolerance for people of varying religious beliefs.

Persecution in Old Europe

The blood shed by thousands during the Middle Ages was a graphic testimony to our founding fathers of the necessity of religious liberty. Consider Henri Arnaud and his band of Waldensians. The Waldensians were a small group of faithful Bible-believing Christians who dared to be different and suffered persecution for it. They refused to accept the decrees of the state-sponsored church in the place of the Word of God. For them, the commands of God were more important than the traditions of men, and in response, the state church sent an army to destroy them.

One spring morning, high on Sugarloaf Mountain, the Waldensians heard shouting far below as Colonel DePerot and his troops made ready for attack. "My lads, we shall sleep up there tonight," was the colonel's proud boast. He even invited the villagers to a public hanging to take place the next day. "Come and see the end of the Waldensians," he proclaimed.

High atop the peak, Waldensian leader Henri Arnaud opened his Bible and read to his company from Psalm 124:2, 3 (NKJV), "If it had not been the Lord who was on our side, when men rose up against us, then they would have swallowed us alive."

DePerot and his 20,000 troops started up the mountain. All went well until the best climbers were ready to reach for the timbers of the mountain fort. At that point, Arnaud's men hailed a volley of stones down upon them. The troops fell back, and Colonel DePerot was wounded and had to ask for refuge in the Waldensian fort. These Christian warriors, whom DePerot had planned to hang, graciously gave him a safe place to sleep for the night—up on the mountain as he had predicted, but certainly not under the conditions he had expected.

The next night, DePerot's soldiers surrounded the fort, but the Waldensians slipped silently away through a dense fog. In the morning, when the soldiers closed in for the kill, they found only empty barracks, except for the one where Colonel DePerot was still sleeping.

Far out of reach on the heights above walked the Waldensians. The soldiers cursed, "Heaven seems to take special interest in preserving these people." But it was not always so. At last came the day when 250 Waldensians were trapped in a cave by soldiers. A fire was built at the opening, and as the oxygen was consumed, the Waldensians sang praises to God until their breath was gone. Along with thousands of others, the Waldensians died rather than compromise their integrity. They accepted martyrdom rather than surrender their liberty.

America's Fading Liberty

Will the religious persecution of the Middle Ages recur in modern America? Will liberty fade in this land of liberty? Jesus stated in John 15:20, "If they have persecuted me, they will also persecute you."

Speaking of the last days, the Saviour added, "Nation shall rise against nation, and kingdom against kingdom: And great earthquakes shall be in divers places, and famines, and pestilences, and fearful sights and great signs shall there be from heaven. But before all these, they shall lay their hands on you, and persecute you, delivering you up to the synagogues and into prisons, being brought before kings and rulers for my name's sake (Luke 21:10-12).

The Saviour continues with these thought-provoking words in verses 15 through 17,

"I will give you a mouth and wisdom, which all your adversaries shall not be able to gainsay nor resist. And ye shall be betrayed both by parents, and brethren, and kinsfolks, and friends; and some of you shall they cause to be put to death. And ye shall be hated of all men for my name's sake."

The prophecies of the book of Revelation add graphic detail regarding these final days of our history. They predict that a giant confederation of evil will seek to compel false worship, and the penalty of resistance will be death. A decree will be passed, evidently worldwide, that "as many as would not worship . . . should be killed" (Revelation 13:15). It couldn't happen here, you say. And yet, you know as well as I do that some of our personal liberties are being subtly undermined. Our daily lives more and more are being affected by legislation. Our privacy is almost a thing of the past. If you watch, you can see that the wedge of intolerance is steadily pushing in.

Deteriorating Social Conditions

The moral fabric of society is falling apart. Divorce is rampant. Crime is of epidemic proportion. Drug abuse is commonplace. Sexual immorality and violence on television have become the norm. There is a cry for the masses to restore "family values" in our society. We are already seeing a backlash against the liberalism and the secular humanism that have had such strong influence in our society. The average citizen recognizes that scrapping our moral values in the '60s and '70s has contributed to the devastating social conditions in our cities in the '80s and '90s.

Due to these deteriorating moral values, conservative Christians have begun working to form a political power block. The cover story blurb on the May 15, 1995, *Time* magazine declares, "Meet Ralph Reed, 33, his Christian Coalition is on a crusade to take over U.S. politics—and it's working." Commenting on the need for religious organizations of all denominations to work together, Ralph Reed states, "No longer burdened by the past, Roman Catholics, Evangelicals, Greek Orthodox, and many religious conservatives from the denominations are forming a new alliance that promises to become among the most powerful and important in the modern political era" (*Politically Incorrect*, p. 16) .

As the moral fabric of society continues to fall apart and natural disasters increase, there will be a swing back to morality, a very strict morality, even a forced morality. It would take only a few major earthquakes or other natural disasters to cause people to ask, "What's wrong? These must be the judgments of God." A natural reaction would be for people to begin to support religious legislation in an attempt to avoid further disaster.

The Final Battle

What is the central issue in earth's final battle over liberty of conscience? Let's go back to the book of Daniel, which was written especially for the time of the end (see Daniel 12:4). In Daniel 3 we read that the Babylonian king, Nebuchadnezzar, set up an image and demanded that people bow down to it in direct defiance of God and the prophecy that he had received in Daniel 2. The image he constructed was a counterfeit of the one he had seen in a prophetic dream. This universal decree compelling worship of a counterfeit image carried with it the penalty of death for all those who did not bow down. Shadrach, Meshach, and Abednego did not bow down. The furnace was heated seven times hotter. Still they refused to yield their conviction to the state decree. They would not accept compelled worship. They confidently declared, "Our God whom we serve is able to deliver us from the burning fiery furnace, and he will deliver us out of thine hand, O king. But if not, be it known unto thee, O king, that we will not serve thy gods, nor worship the golden image which thou hast set up" (Daniel 3:17, 18).

Shadrach, Meshach, and Abednego were roughly thrown into the fiery furnace. Miraculously, they were not consumed. As the king looked in, he saw a fourth Being in their midst. Immediately, he sensed that this supernatural being was the Son of God. The divine Protector, the Lord

Jesus Christ, was with His people in their greatest time of trial.

Once again, in the last days of earth's history, a counterfeit image will be established—a substitute sign of allegiance, a false mark of loyalty. According to Revelation 13:12, the issue will be worship. A church-state power will attempt to compel the consciences of men. The final conflict will be over the law of God. This issue is quite clearly defined in Revelation 12:17: "The dragon was wroth with the woman, and went to make war with the remnant of her seed, which keep the commandments of God, and have the testimony of Jesus Christ." The dragon symbolizes Satan. A pure, undefiled woman represents God's church. Satan is angry with the church and makes war with the remnant of her seed, the last part of the church, the church in our day. And why is he angry? God's people keep His commandments. From the beginning of his rebellion, the law of God has been the target of his anger. It still will be in the final conflict.

But notice, there are two targets of the devil's anger. He's angry because God's people keep God's commandments, but also because they have the testimony of Jesus. In the fourteenth chapter, God's people in the final days are described this way, "Here are they that keep the commandments of God, and the faith of Jesus" (Revelation 14:12).

The commandments of God and the faith of Jesus go together. And the faith of Jesus is also a target of Satan's anger. In fact, we're told that the forces of evil in the last bitter conflict will "make war with the Lamb" (Revelation 17:14). That's Jesus, the Lamb of God.

What was it that caused persecution in the days of the apostles? It was the fact that they were preaching Jesus. They were preaching salvation by faith in Christ. They said there was no other way to be saved. But the religious leaders of that day wanted to save themselves by their own elaborate system of salvation by works. They didn't want to admit that it was useless. And so man-made traditions of the Pharisees were pitted against the simple teaching of Christ.

In the final day, the issue will be the same—man-made laws against the laws of God. Salvation by works against salvation by faith. And as a last resort, salvation by legislation will come into the picture. Do you see what we're going to face?

In his book *The New World Order*, page 236, Pat Robertson emphasizes this thought. "Laws in America that demanded a day of rest from incessant commerce have been nullified as a violation of the separation of church and state. In modern America, shopping centers, malls and stores of every description carry on their frantic pace seven days a week as an outright insult to God and His plan. Only those policies that can be shown to have a clearly secular purpose are recognized." Robertson argues that a godly state must have religious laws at its heart. Can you see how this attitude can easily lead to intolerance? Can you see how the rights of the minority can be trampled on for the good of the majority?

Compelling Conscience

Dr. Stanley Milgram, a psychologist, conducted experiments to discover just how far a person will go in causing pain to another individual when he is ordered to do so. His experiments contain significant lessons for those of us living at end time. The results of these studies are not only extremely significant, but mighty frightening.

The experiments were conducted some years ago at Yale

University. Advertisements were placed in New Haven, Connecticut, newspapers asking for 500 male volunteers to participate in a study of memory. As men responded, appointments were set up. When a volunteer arrived at the laboratory for his appointment, a second man would arrive at the same time, posing as another volunteer. Actually, the second man was an actor hired to help with the experiment.

The two men were told that they were participating in a study of the effects of punishment on learning. One was to be the teacher and the other the learner. They were allowed to draw to see which role each would play, but drawing was rigged so that the actor would always play the role of the learner. The teacher and learner were in separate rooms, but the teacher could observe that the learner was hooked up to what seemed to be an electrode. The teacher was instructed to administer an electric shock to the learner whenever he made a mistake and to increase the voltage with each new mistake.

The actor, who played the part of the student, would not actually receive any shocks at all, but when the voltage was raised to 75 volts, he would act like he had been mildly hurt. At 120 volts he would begin to complain, and at 150 volts he would demand that the experiment cease. If the "teacher" continued to administer shocks, at 285 volts the actor would let out an agonized scream.

Many "teachers" would begin to protest when they realized they were injuring another person but would be ordered to go on because the experiment must continue. Many of them would continue giving shocks up to the highest levels, no matter how much the actor begged to be released.

Now you may think that anybody in his or her right

mind wouldn't even give the first shock, but the terrible truth is that almost two-thirds of the participants were willing to go to almost any length when commanded to do so. Many went all the way up to 450 volts, no matter how hard the victim begged to be released. Why did they do it? Did they want to? No. Was it because of the aggressiveness or hostility in their nature? No. They did it simply because a man in a laboratory coat told them to do it. That white coat represented to them authority. No police badge, no gun, just a white coat.

The volunteers were interviewed afterward and asked why they had continued giving the shocks. Almost invariably the answer was the same—it was simply that they had been ordered to do it. Many believed that what they were doing was very wrong, but they didn't have the courage to refuse to go on. By the time the experiment was over, they had justified their conduct on the basis that they were simply following orders. They were more concerned about how good a job they had done.

Why didn't they just walk out if they thought it was wrong? Simple reasons—they wanted to be polite. They were helping science. They had made a commitment. It would be awkward.

Yes, it is very awkward to disobey an order. And I wonder if you see the frightening implications. The horrors of Nazi Germany were not all committed by a man named Hitler. They were carried out by subordinates at all levels who were just following orders. Even the notorious Eichman, who was sickened when he visited the gas chambers, insisted that he was just a man at a desk shuffling papers and following orders.

Here is the precise issue in the last days of earth's history. The issue is one of authority. The issue is one of obedience.

The issue is one of allegiance. One group of men and women allow others to mold their consciences. One group of men and women accept the authority of man. They obey the religious leaders of their day. Another group of men and women are fiercely loyal to Christ. They are totally committed to Christ. They proclaim with the apostles of old, "We ought to obey God rather than men" (Acts 5:29). They would rather die than disobey their Creator. They cry out with the Bible prophet, Isaiah, "To the law and to the testimony: if they speak not according to this word, it is because there is no light in them" (Isaiah 8:20).

They are not rabble-rousers. They are not leaders of some revolt in society. They are not social misfits or political activists. They are committed Christians dedicated to following Christ and the testimony of the Bible. They have chosen to be obedient to God's commandments rather than accept the traditions of men. They are determinedly loyal to God. They will not surrender their conscientious biblical convictions for the teachings of compromising religious leaders.

Scores of men and women are going to go the easy, crossless way. The majority will conform. But there will be those who are loyal, those who are faithful, those who would rather die than yield their conscientious convictions.

God is calling you to be faithful to Him. Whatever He calls us to do, He gives us the power to do it. When church and state unite, when man-made compromise is forced upon Christianity, when faithful men and women cannot buy or sell, when liberty fades in America and the death penalty hangs over our heads, Christ speaks with a still, small voice and says, "Do not yield. I will be with you."

> Do you long to live in a land where there is no pain, sickness, or death? What is that land like? Is heaven a real place? Or is it a vague spirit world or a grand delusion? If heaven is a real place, what will we do there for millions of years? If a real Christ is coming to take us to our real home, what's it like? Find out as you read this last chapter.

CHAPTER

TWELVE

The World of Tomorrow

After fifteen years of searching for the missing pharaoh in the Valley of the Kings, Howard Carter was almost ready to give up his quest in the year 1922. He had invested a good part of his life digging near the monuments and tombs that others had excavated before him. Thirty-three royal tombs had been discovered in the Valley, but all had been plundered by thieves. The experts concluded that this burial ground of the Pharaohs had yielded all its secrets.

But Howard Carter wasn't convinced. He insisted that the tomb of a boy king named Tutankhamen had to be there—somewhere. He'd found a cup, pieces of gold foil, and pottery jars all bearing Tutankhamen's name. All his excavations, however, had come up empty, so Carter's sponsor, Lord Carnarvon, finally declared that he could no longer finance the archaeologist's expeditions.

Carter desperately pleaded for one last chance. If he didn't find the tomb, he said, he'd pay for the work himself. Lord Carnarvon agreed to give him just one more opportunity.

In early November, Carter's workmen uncovered a staircase. The staircase led to a door. Examining it, Carter noticed the seal of the jackal god. That seal was affixed to royal tombs. It had not yet been broken. "It was a thrilling moment," he wrote later, "for an excavator in that valley of unutterable silence."

Carter cabled his sponsor and asked him to come to the site. The morning after Lord Carnarvon arrived, Carter cut a hole through the doorway. It was November 26, 1922, the most wonderful day of his life. He lifted a candle and peered in.

"For a moment," Carter wrote, "I was dumb-struck with amazement." He saw "strange animals, statues, and gold—everywhere the gold of gold." In that instant, the archaeologist felt himself transported to another time and another place, radically different from anything he had ever known.

Lord Carnarvon could hardly stand the suspense. He asked, "Howard, Howard, can you see anything?"

And Carter, trying to describe the greatest archaeological discovery in history, could only say, "Yes, wonderful things."

Until that moment, no one had imagined the staggering wealth, the dazzling art, or the royal glory that lay hidden in the sand. In all, more than 5,000 treasures were found in the tomb. It took Carter more than nine years to remove and transfer them to the Cairo Museum. And this left everyone with a question. Why were all these priceless items buried with Tutankhamen? Buried in the dark, sealed in an inner chamber where no human eye could enjoy them. What was the point?

Another Ruler

Let's contrast the fate of this boy-king with another ruler in Egypt, about 200 years earlier. This was Moses, whom Providence and a desperate mother placed in a basket on the River Nile. The Pharaoh's daughter found and adopted the child but let his real Hebrew mother raise him.

For nearly twelve years, Jochabed taught Moses to obey and trust the God of heaven. Then the boy was taken from his humble home to the royal palace to officially become the son of the princess.

Pharaoh decided to make him his adopted grandson. He decided to make him successor to the throne. He saw to it that the boy was properly educated for his high position. Moses received the best civil and military training the court of Pharaoh could offer.

All steps led him to the glory of Egypt's throne. It was then the center of the civilized world; all its wealth and influence and power would lie at his feet. It was his for the taking—if he would just give his allegiance to Aton and Osiris instead of the God of heaven. Pharaoh's palace would be his home. The Valley of the Kings would provide a final resting place. His body, too, would be entombed with the finest treasures of the land.

But no archaeologist's spade has ever broken through the tomb of Moses. And no expedition ever will. Because no tomb was ever built.

Moses made one of history's most critical decisions. It's recorded in Hebrews 11:24, 25: "By faith Moses, when he was come to years, refused to be called the son of Pharaoh's daughter; choosing rather to suffer affliction with the people of God, than to enjoy the pleasures of sin for a season."

Moses identified himself with the suffering Hebrews, the

slaves. Their cause became his cause. And so God used him to bring his nation to freedom and to the promised land.

A Better Future

Moses looked beyond the palaces, beyond the gilded chariots and ivory furniture. He didn't want to be buried with such relics. He didn't want to be encased in gold. Moses chose a different fate: to become the son of the mighty King, the God of heaven, and serve Him.

Many years later, Moses died alone on top of Mount Nebo, gazing out at the Promised Land he would never enter. No royal fanfare, no elaborate funeral, no glorious tomb.

Had it been a fair exchange? A life of struggle with the wandering children of Israel for the riches and power of Egypt's throne? An apparently insignificant ending for a place in the Valley of the Kings?

To answer that, let's go back to the first question we raised. Let's go back to the tomb of Tutankhamen. Why did the Egyptians seal all these treasures with a dead king?

The answer involves their idea of how to prepare for the afterlife. The ancients believed they could provide the deceased with the accessories that would enable them to go on living in the style to which they became accustomed in this life. They believed the Pharaohs had to travel first-class in the journey from life to the mysterious world of the dead.

That's why Tutankhamen's tomb was stuffed with beautiful furniture, exquisitely carved utensils, elaborate chests, and vessels of oil. The Pharaohs did all within their power to make immortality a luxurious affair.

No one supplied these things or hammered out a gilded death mask for Moses. But let's discover his ultimate fate.

What does the Bible teach regarding the wisdom of Moses' choice?

We gain some remarkable insight from the little book of Jude. "But even the archangel Michael, when he was disputing with the devil about the body of Moses, did not dare to bring a slanderous accusation against him, but said, 'The Lord rebuke you!' " (Jude 9, NKJV).

After Moses died, our Lord Himself debated with Satan regarding resurrecting the body of Moses. Now, of course, Satan desired Moses to remain locked in his grave. But our Lord raised Moses bodily from the grave as a type of all those who will be resurrected when Jesus returns. Scripture is not describing some disembodied spirit or immortal soul of Moses. Moses was literally, bodily, resurrected from the dead, just like we will be when Jesus comes.

Let's fast forward time through the centuries.

We go to the top of a certain mountain in Judea where Jesus is transfigured before three of His disciples. His garments become dazzling white; his face seems to shine like the sun. Then two figures appear with him: Moses and Elijah. The one, Moses, resurrected from the grave, and the other, Elijah, translated to heaven without seeing death. Moses represents those who will be resurrected bodily when Jesus comes. Elijah represents those translated without seeing death. And they're talking with their friend, Jesus, giving Him encouragement.

This brief scene shows us Moses' remarkable fate. Apparently our heavenly Father just couldn't resist taking Moses to heaven ahead of time, before that hour when the Bible says all the righteous will be taken up to heaven with Christ at His second coming.

So what fate did Moses find at the end of his long, hard

journey? He found a better Promised Land. He found himself face-to-face with Jesus Christ, in his Father's house.

Yes, I'd say Moses made a good exchange, what do you think? I'd rather be talking with Jesus than lying in a gilded sarcophagus—no matter how many jewels or how much gold surrounded me. I'd rather be walking in my Father's house than lying with the wealth of the pharaohs.

Moses saw, by faith, that all the razzle and dazzle in this world is nothing compared to the vastness of God's riches in eternity. He was one of those great men of faith celebrated in the book of Hebrews, whose eyes were fixed on "the city with foundations, whose architect and builder is God."

The New Jerusalem

The apostle John describes that heavenly city in the book of Revelation. What he saw in vision was so dazzling that he used every metaphor, every shining gem he could think of, to try to express its glory. He called it "a bride adorned for her husband." Its gates appear to be giant pearls; all its streets are gold. The River of Life flows down its center, clear as crystal, bordered by the Tree of Life bearing a dozen different fruits, and whose leaves are for "the healing of the nations."

This is the place that Moses looked forward to, a place where every sorrow and every tear is wiped away. The many beautiful mansions our Father has prepared for the living, not the dead, are there. The prophet Isaiah pictures a land where the blind see, the lame leap, and the dumb hear, where the lion and the lamb lie down together. It's a place where there's no sickness, no crime, no dying, no exhaustion at the end of every week.

In His magnificent Sermon on the Mount, Jesus declared in Matthew 5:5: "Blessed are the meek: for they shall inherit the earth."

The apostle Peter adds in 2 Peter, chapter 3, verse 13 (NIV): "But in keeping with his promise we are looking forward to a new heaven and a new earth, the home of righteousness."

Heaven is not some fairy-tale world—not some world of ethereal spiritlike ghosts and goblins. Heaven is a real place. God created this earth to be inhabited by healthy and happy and holy beings. According to the Bible, this earth will be recreated in Edenic splendor. It will become the perfect home of the saved after the New Jerusalem descends from heaven (see Revelation 21:1, 2).

But some have wondered what we will do in such a perfect world. Most of our activities here on this earth revolve around dealing with the kinds of problems that won't exist in the new earth. Will we just hang around idly strumming golden harps?

Well, first of all, we have to get beyond this idea of some wispy bank of clouds as being heaven. The heavenly city— the New Jerusalem—the cosmic control center of the universe, will actually become the capital of none other than planet Earth. In Revelation, John saw it "coming down from God out of heaven." John saw a new and perfect Earth where sin no longer exists, "for the first heaven and the first earth had passed away." This Earth will be completely renewed, returned to its perfect state in a new Eden. It'll be a glorious new frontier to explore.

Heavenly Activity

How will we keep busy? The truth of the matter is that in the earth made new we'll be free to experience life as it was originally meant to be. There's so much to hold us back now. We waste so much energy in resentment and anxiety and guilt. And sometimes we just go in circles. But in the earth made new, we'll finally be let loose. We'll finally be able to release our creativity and fulfill our dreams.

Have you ever been caught up in designing your "perfect dream house?" Remember how excited you were? Remember how alive you felt? You imagined this cozy little study on the second floor or that sparkling swimming pool by the patio. With a shaky economy and financial pressures, a dream home may seem impossible to you. You may live in a tenement apartment in one of America's major cities. Home ownership may seem to be out of your reach.

Isaiah tells us that the new earth will be a place where those "someday" plans become a reality. Listen to Isaiah 65:21, 22: "They will build houses and dwell in them; they will plant vineyards and eat their fruit . . . my chosen ones will long enjoy the works of their hands" (NIV).

A number of years ago, our family lived in Sterling, Massachusetts. Each year we had a large garden. One of the great joys of my life was returning from my evangelistic meetings and working in my garden. No food tasted so good as the food that came out of my garden. Green beans and tomatoes and corn and strawberries and raspberries were mouth-watering!

In the glorious earth made new, we'll enjoy food grown in our own gardens. What an unimaginable taste delight! Perfect taste buds, perfect soil, perfect climate, and perfect crops. I can hardly wait for this gourmet feast!

Our hands and our minds were designed by God to build and create and work out our dreams. Immortality isn't immobility. We'll be producing things then that are inconceivable to us now.

Heavenly Reunions

But think of another dimension to life in the heavenly city. Think of all the times you've had to say "goodbye," all the times you've had to say, "if we only had one more time together." One of the greatest joys for people in heaven will be other people.

There's so much that keeps us apart on earth now, so much that keeps us relating on a superficial level. But in the earth made new, all the barriers will come down. We can develop rich and satisfying relationships with an infinite variety of friends.

You know, I'd love to talk to Moses. I'd like to ask him what it was like walking through the Red Sea, or, "Moses, what was it like climbing Mt. Sinai in the thunder and smoke?" I'd also like to meet David and Daniel, or can you imagine spending an afternoon with Peter or John and listening to them tell about the day Lazarus walked out of his tomb?

As an evangelist, I'd like to talk to some of the great men of God like John Wesley or Dwight Moody and hear their stories.

I'm sure there are people you'd like to see too. Perhaps there's a son or daughter who was taken from you by death, and you can't wait to throw your arms around them again. Heaven is about reunion. It's about getting together in ways we never would have believed before. It's about wonderful, stimulating relationships.

And the greatest, most exciting reunion of all will be the day that we walk up to Jesus Christ, that we see Him at last face-to-face, and converse with the One whose presence is so brilliant it makes the sun seem unnecessary in the new earth. And to join our voices in a vast chorus of ecstatic praise. You know, it's almost too much to think about.

Meeting Your Best Friend

I've imagined myself meeting Jesus in heaven. Gently, He places His nail-scarred hand on my shoulder. All the reminders of sin are gone except one—the nail prints in His hands. His compassionate, understanding eyes reveal that He knows everything about me, yet He loves me still. The One who knows me best loves me most. In words of tenderest compassion, He gently inquires, "Can we spend some time together?" My heart beats with eager anticipation. The Creator of the universe, the Redeemer of the world wants to spend time with me!

As we begin walking down a grassy tree-lined lane, crossing a crystal-clear babbling brook, Jesus kindly says, "Bend over, Mark, drink some of this life-giving water." This water from the River of Life flowing from the throne of God is invigorating, it's life-giving.

He leads me to the Tree of Life, placing its fruit directly into my hands. As I eat it, I sense a tingling sensation of health. I've never felt so good.

Passing through fields of magnificent flowers, Jesus simply asks, "Is there any more I can do for you? My whole life is totally dedicated to making you happy!"

He calls me by a special name—a pet name—known only to the two of us. It's our special secret together. He satisfies all my desires. He meets all my needs. I've never been in the presence of one so totally committed to my happiness before. I've never felt so accepted—so secure—so loved.

He stretches out His nail-scarred hands, gently saying with a tear in His eye, "If you ever doubt my love, remember these."

All I can do is fall at His feet and worship Him. His love

breaks my heart forever. All I can do is bow before Him singing, "Worthy, worthy is the Lamb that was slain to receive wisdom and glory and honor forever."

How can you possibly turn your back on One who loves you so much? How can you possibly walk away from Him? He longs to take a walk with you through eternity. He longs to reveal the mysteries of His love. He longs to hold you in His arms safe and secure forever. This is no dream. This is no make-believe tale. It's reality today—right now. This moment I invite you into the security of His love forever.

A time is coming soon when that other time and place will burst on this planet in a blaze of glory. Howard Carter's discovery of King Tutankhamen's tomb is just a hint of what's going to happen to us. Staring through that hole in the doorway, he was dumbstruck—"Wonderful things . . . the glint of gold everywhere." Another world suddenly came to life at his fingertips.

Imagine what it'll be like to see heaven itself, Jesus Christ Himself, descend to this planet at His second coming. I want to be part of that great reunion. I want my life aimed toward that eternal glory that outweighs all my present difficulties. I want to put my life in the hands of Jesus Christ, the Saviour, today, so I can see Him face-to-face tomorrow.

Isn't that the deepest desire in your heart as well? Let's determine to be ready for that wonderful reunion. That way we'll have the privilege of living, not just beyond 2000, but forever.